AJAX
THE KEA DOG

AJAX
THE KEA DOG

A working dog's life in the high country

COREY MOSEN
with Nicola McCloy

ALLEN&UNWIN

SYDNEY · MELBOURNE · AUCKLAND · LONDON

First published in 2018

Copyright © Corey Mosen, 2018

Photography by Corey Mosen, unless otherwise
credited on the image or on page 256

Allen & Unwin
Level 3, 228 Queen Street
Auckland 1010, New Zealand
Phone: (64 9) 377 3800
Email: info@allenandunwin.com
Web: www.allenandunwin.co.nz

83 Alexander Street
Crows Nest NSW 2065, Australia
Phone: (61 2) 8425 0100

A catalogue record for this book is available from
the National Library of New Zealand.

ISBN 978 1 76063 361 5

Design by Kate Barraclough
Set in Adobe Caslon Pro
Printed and bound in China by Hang Tai Printing
Company Limited
10 9 8 7 6 5 4 3 2 1

To my amazing wife, Sarah, and my twins, Zara and Leo. May the adventures of Ajax inspire more fun and exploration in the years to come.

CONTENTS

AJAX THE KEA DOG

Me and Ajax in Kahurangi National Park.

A soft, low light wakes me. I take a moment to work out where I am. The rowdy chorus of birds tells me that it's early morning and I'm in my tent above the bushline in the Kahurangi National Park. As the pink blaze of sunrise slowly filters inside, I wriggle out of my sleeping bag and open the zip at the front of my tent.

Lying there in the vestibule is my trusty companion and workmate, Ajax. At home, he's not a big fan of mornings, and when we're out in the bush he's not that different. He looks at me without moving and I can tell he's thinking, *just a few minutes more . . .* But we've got work to do.

I reach over and open the front of the vestibule, and give Ajax a nudge until he gets up and grudgingly goes outside. He sits and waits patiently while I get dressed and pull on my boots. Once I'm out and have the billy boiling for my coffee, it's breakfast time for Ajax.

He's happy to have just a couple of handfuls of biscuits, but on special occasions he'll opt for a feed of fresh goat to start the day. I can't say it would be my favourite choice of breakfast, but Ajax loves it. In fact, he loves it so much that sometimes he'll hide the leftovers from the previous night's goat dinner and wander off to find them in the morning so he can have them for breakfast. On those days, I'm usually relieved if it's been a bit cool overnight and the meat has been kept chilled by Mother Nature. After a warm night, Ajax's favourite breakfast can be pretty stinky.

While Ajax is distracted by his breakfast, I'll have my coffee while I watch the sky brighten, the coming day revealing a bush-clad valley below us through which a wild river runs. From there I scan across to the high plateau on the other side of the valley. Our goal for today is to head down into the valley, through the river, up the hill, across the plateau and down the other side in search of kea nests. As workplaces go, this one has a pretty good view.

Breakfast finished, I pack the tent down and prepare to get moving for the day. Now he's eaten, Ajax is wide awake and excited to get going. Once I've got my gear sorted out, Ajax gets his hi-vis coat and his muzzle on and we're ready to roll.

We set off down the mountain and into the dappled light of the moss-laden beech forest. Ajax happily follows me as I make my way among the trees, heading for a spot where I know there are likely to be kea nests. Actually, I say that Ajax follows me, but at the start of the day he's usually so excited that he'll take off ahead of me, and he'll have to keep either doubling back or turning around to make sure he's going the right way! That lasts until about lunchtime, after which he slows down a bit; then he'll be just behind me for the rest of the day.

As we're walking, Ajax is always scoping out what's happening around us, having a good sniff here and there to make sure he's not missing anything. If he does find a smell that he's interested in, he'll head off in the direction of whatever he's found. He never does this without making sure that I know where he's going, though, and that I'm following him. When he's on the scent of something he has some pretty classic pointing behaviours, and I know him so well I know exactly what he's trying to tell me.

If it's a kea nest, he'll sit down in front of it and wait until I get there. One of the key ways I can tell that he knows he's found what I'm after is that he looks really chuffed with himself. He absolutely loves working, and is never happier than when he's found an active or recently used nest. Even after years of tracking these birds, he still gets a real kick when he actually finds them.

When I get to the spot that he's trying to show me, I give him a big pat and make a real fuss of him. He loves nothing more than being told he's a good boy! That's all the reward he needs to keep him working and following the scent of one of our smartest, funniest, most amazing and, sadly, very rare native birds.

Ajax probably knows more about kea than most people do. One thing's for sure—he certainly knows what they smell like. And that's without him coming face to face with the birds very often. Mostly, he just scents their nests or their general locations before letting me know where they are.

Once I've given him plenty of praise, he has no further interest in the birds and will just wander off to the nearest piece of dry ground, preferably in the shade of a tree on a hot day. He knows that I'm going to be a while, so he'll make the most of the opportunity to have a bit of a snooze.

While Ajax is napping, I'll look into the kea nest to see if anyone's home. If there's a bird in there on her nest, she'll usually just sit and watch me as I set up cameras to monitor her movements and those of her chicks. If the chicks are big enough to cope with their mother being away from the nest, I'll also band the mother bird and take her measurements. If I'm out of sight for too long, Ajax might wander across and wait at the entrance to the nest and have a little whine to let me know he's still there. But usually he'll just take the opportunity for a good rest.

Seeing a sleeping dog is sometimes too tempting for an inquisitive adult kea. They've been known to strut right up to Ajax, circle around him a couple of times, then either peck him on the soft pads of his feet or try to pinch a tuft of fur from his tail. For Ajax, this kind of treatment is all part of the job, and he'll just lie there and let them do it.

Once we've made our way down the hill, checked out a few nests and waded across the river—Ajax is a keen swimmer, so he often beats me to the other side—I decide it's time for lunch and a chance to dry out in the warmth of the midday sun. I lower Ajax's muzzle and we both sit for a couple of minutes enjoying the sun's rays on our wet legs.

Because he's had quite a big breakfast, Ajax doesn't really get hungry during the day, but I often share a bit of my sandwich with him and that always makes him happy. He's usually thirsty though, so he wanders back down to the river and has a good, long drink while I sort out my pack and get ready to start climbing back up through the bush. Once Ajax's muzzle is back on we head straight up into the trees again.

The afternoon goes along the same way as the morning. The pair of us amble through the bush and climb over rocks, checking out kea nests as we retrace our path to the spot where we left the truck a couple of days ago.

Once Ajax realises that we're nearly back to the truck, he steps up his pace a little bit. He knows we're nearly done for the day, and I can tell he's happy with another good day's work done.

As we finally make our way around the last corner, his tail is wagging fast and he races across to the truck, almost tripping over himself. Once I take his muzzle and coat off he knows that he has finished work for the day.

When I open the door of the truck, Ajax bounces straight into the back and makes himself comfortable for the ride home—never mind that I still have to sort out all our gear. If he could drive, I reckon he'd probably have the key in the ignition and be gone before I'd even managed to stow our gear and shut the door! If he could drive, though, it would entirely interfere with his regular ride home—lying in the back, sound asleep, probably dreaming of birds. That is until the moment I turn the truck into our driveway, then he bounces up, wide awake and more than a little happy to be home.

No sooner have I let him out of the truck than he'll be off inside to say hi to my wife, Sarah, and to check whether our rapidly growing twins have left home yet. Then he'll plop himself down on the living-room floor waiting for someone—anyone—to pat him and make a bit of a fuss of him. Another hard day's work out in the field tracking kea is over, and his transformation from rugged, outdoors conservation warrior to much-loved family pet is complete.

Me, Sarah and Ajax, posing for a photo
the day before the twins arrived.

CHAPTER ONE
LIFE BEFORE AJAX

Before Ajax, I had a job with DOC in the Hawke's Bay. This kiwi was the first one I ever caught and handled. PHOTO BY RHYS BURNS

I've been Ajax's sidekick for so long now that it's hard to remember what life was like before he was around to keep me company in the bush—letting me know where kea nests are, throwing a sook when I'm up rock climbing, making me laugh with his daft antics, grossing me out with his bad farts and letting me know when it's time to go to bed. But I did have a life before Ajax—one that led me to meeting a funny little dog in Westport in 2011.

I've always been really into animals. As a kid, when Mum would take me and my brother Bradley to the library, I would get out piles of books about animals. One day, I was sitting at the table reading while I waited for my brother to check his books out. A lady saw me and said to Mum, 'Do you realise that every book your son has chosen is about animals?' Mum looked over at me, and the lady added, 'You need to foster that, because you never know where that might lead.' Mum reckons she's never forgotten that conversation with a stranger. And that stranger turned out to be very right.

I also loved watching *Our World* on TV—Mum used to video every episode for me and I'd watch them over and over again. Then, when I was about eight, Mum bought a set of the *World Book Encyclopedia*. She reckons they were the best thing she ever bought. Instead of reading story books, I would sit on the toilet and read the encyclopedia, meticulously working my way through the alphabet and looking up all the different animals and birds, quietly taking in the details.

According to Mum, I'd often come home with injured birds

that I'd rescued from some scrape or other. In Whanganui, where I was brought up, there was a woman called Dawn Morton who was known as the Bird Lady, and we'd sometimes take the injured birds out to her.

We'd often go to Christchurch for our holidays, because that's where my mum's parents lived. My grandfather was friends with a man who was very involved with Orana Wildlife Park, and occasionally he would get us free tickets. We also went to Willowbank Wildlife Reserve from time to time, and I would be in my element. And if we visited any other cities, we'd always go to the zoo and see the animals.

Looking back now, it seems strange that we never had a dog when I was a kid, especially given that Ajax has become such a big part of my life. The first time I remember having anything to do with dogs, it wasn't a great experience. I was walking my usual way home from school when a Dobermann crossed my path. It was big. (Well, much bigger than me.) The dog stopped and eyed me up. I was scared. I didn't know what to do, but I decided I needed to get away from it as fast as I could. So I started running.

But when I started running, the dog started running too. It didn't take long for it to catch up with me. It jumped up and knocked me to the ground, then landed on top of me. I lay there in fright while it had a good sniff and a bit of a lick of me, then it wandered off. It didn't bite me or anything—I reckon it just thought that I was playing with it. For a while after that I used to take a different route home, but thankfully the experience didn't put me off dogs.

The next time I came into close contact with a dog was when I rescued one. We were visiting my uncle at the air force base at Wigram, near Christchurch—once again we were down there on holiday. My brother and one of my cousins and I got caught out in a massive crazy downpour, and we found this little dog that was soaking wet. It was huddled next to a clothing bin and it was shivering uncontrollably. Looking back now, I think it probably had hypothermia. I just knew that we had to help it.

I was the smallest one there, so my brother and my cousin boosted me up until I could climb in through the flap of the clothing bin. I gathered up a bunch of clothes, then knocked on the flap so they knew to pull me back out again. Once I was safely out of the bin, I wrapped the little dog up in the clothes I'd managed to nick (for a good cause). We took it back to my uncle's house on the base and he managed to find the dog's owner and reunite them.

When my brother was older he got a dog, a bull terrier, and I loved hanging out with him. I used to look after him when my brother was away. That dog bit me a couple of times, though. Once he grabbed a chunk of my arse and wouldn't let go. Another time, he jumped up and dragged me down by the fleshy part under my arm. It wasn't aggressive—he just thought I was one of his dog buddies.

Even though I didn't have a dog of my own, I had a lot more to do with them when I was growing up than I did with kea. The first time I remember seeing a kea I was quite young. We were on a family trip to the West Coast and we stopped at Arthur's Pass. These birds landed on my nana's car and started fearlessly chewing up the windscreen wipers with their hooked beaks. I remember thinking, *these birds are cool*, though I'm pretty sure that Nana thought quite the opposite . . .

When I was at school, I didn't really know what I wanted to do when I grew up. I thought I'd quite like to be a vet, but then I went and worked at a vet's practice over the school holidays and it was really shit! Killing old dogs or chopping their nuts off, pulling kittens out of cats, cleaning up piss . . . it wasn't what I'd pictured. Being a vet—especially in towns and cities—is mainly dealing with companion animals, and that wasn't what I wanted to do.

While I made up my mind about what to do instead, university seemed the obvious place to go. I enrolled at Massey in Palmerston North and studied zoology. That's the science of pretty much everything to do with animals, including ecology, biology, physiology and psychology.

While I studied, I worked as a builder to help pay the bills.

Towards the end of my degree, I was able to organise my papers to fit around the days I wanted to work. The added bonus of this was that I had a job to go to when I finished my degree.

I kept building when I finished university, so I could save money to go travelling. My first big overseas trip after I graduated was four months spent travelling around Europe. It was a good break after having worked and studied constantly for the previous few years.

After I came home, I went building again and did some more study. This time I took some papers in captive management, to qualify me to get a job in a zoo.

I was back living in Whanganui, working as a builder, but on the weekends I would drive up to New Plymouth to work at the Brooklands Zoo. I'd always wanted to work with monkeys, and now I got my wish. The only problem was that I found my job at the zoo a bit boring, because I spent my days chopping food and cleaning up poo.

Zoos get a bad rap from some people, but one thing I learned from working in one is that they have a very important role in terms of education. They provide a valuable way for kids to engage with nature. Once kids get to *see* endangered animals, rather than just read or hear about them, they care so much more.

The main reason working at the zoo didn't capture my imagination was that I really wanted to be out in the wild. That got me thinking, *what's New Zealand's equivalent of a monkey? The kea!* Their personalities, as well as their behaviour and family structure, are a lot like that of a monkey. The way they mob up together and cruise around in gangs causing mischief together is very primate-like. They're incredibly intelligent and super adaptable. They'll explore and exploit anything in their path to find out whether it's edible, usable or fun.

I reckon they're one of the world's most intelligent birds. There are numerous examples of them outsmarting humans. Down in Fiordland there are stoat traps running in lines up and down the mountains, and the kea have worked out how to poke sticks inside the trap to set them off. They seem to love the noise the traps make when they're triggered. More than that, they like the fact that setting the traps off breaks the eggs (used as bait) inside them. They have worked out how to poke sticks into the eggs, dragging the whites and yolks out through the mesh of the traps. So not only do the traps provide them with entertainment, they also provide them with a feed.

Kea learn to be unafraid of humans if they hang around them long enough. They can be super entertaining to watch while they get into mischief. But they can also be really annoying if it's your stuff they're nicking and demolishing! They're totally the monkeys of the bird world.

I've since learned that there's scientific evidence to back up my kea–monkey comparison. Scientists have found that kea have a behavioural and cognitive profile that's really similar to both cetaceans—that is, dolphins and whales—and primates.

One thing that quickly became obvious to me was that if I wanted to work with kea, I wouldn't be spending the rest of my life in a zoo. There are only a few kea in captivity in New Zealand. To have a kea in captivity, a zoo or aviary has to have a permit from the Department of Conservation (DOC), and to get that you have to prove that you can provide the kea with a high standard of management and housing. One of the key components of this is providing the birds with an unpredictable, enriched environment where there's plenty of stimulus for them.

DOC controls the numbers of kea held in captivity very tightly. In 2002, there were just over 100 birds in captivity, but that has been reduced to around 50 through natural attrition over time.

It's easy to feel sorry for these captive birds, but they do serve several purposes. They can raise public awareness of the plight of kea in the wild. By seeing and interacting with the birds, people who might not otherwise take an interest can learn about them and become more engaged with their protection. It's a chance to foster tolerance and understanding for a species that has been seen as a pest for many years. Captive birds also give us a great opportunity for research, which can help us better understand kea behaviour. And they provide a bit of an insurance policy in case anything should happen to the wild population.

At this stage, there are no protocols for releasing captive-bred kea into the wild. That's largely because they need to learn so much from their parents when they grow up in their natural environment, and they don't learn the same things when they grow up in a zoo. With many birds a lot of their behaviour is innate, so if you put them back out there they'd be fine, but kea behaviour is learned from their parents and so they probably wouldn't survive if released into the wild.

Anyway, once I decided that my future lay with kea, I started hassling everyone I knew who had anything to do with them so that I could get a foot in the door. I volunteered at Pukaha Mount Bruce, the wildlife centre in the Wairarapa, then I managed to get on a few volunteer trips in the South Island for DOC and the Kea Conservation Trust. I had to pay to get there, but we were supplied with food and accommodation when we were working.

On the first trip I went on, in 2008, I caught my first-ever kea. We were up in the Mātukituki Valley, in the Mount Aspiring National Park. I was pretty stoked, as it was the first wild kea I'd ever held. But it didn't go that well.

The woman who was measuring and banding the bird was engrossed in the task at hand. I didn't want to panic her, so I simply said, 'Ummm, just to let you know, this kea's biting me. But it's OK, you do what you're doing.'

In reality, things were a bit more serious. The bird had bitten into the meaty bit at the bottom of my thumb and was grinding and twisting away at the flesh. What made things worse for me was that before we'd caught the kea, I'd seen it feeding on a bloated dead sheep.

Afterwards, I spent ages cleaning out the wound with alcohol and hoping like hell I didn't end up getting some sort of poisoning off the maggoty old sheep the bird had been eating. The scar that it left on my thumb was a real souvenir of my first catch. Since then I've had heaps of kea bites, but I remind myself that when I was a builder the injuries were a lot worse!

The creature I'm holding in this shot in Western Australia is a red-tailed phascogale (a rare marsupial). PHOTO BY ROB HILL

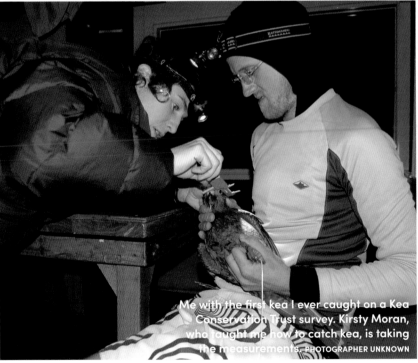

Me with the first kea I ever caught on a Kea Conservation Trust survey. Kirsty Moran, who taught me how to catch kea, is taking the measurements. PHOTOGRAPHER UNKNOWN

Me checking out a kea nest in Nelson Lakes National Park. PHOTO BY BRADLEY MOSEN

A juvenile kea takes flight in Mount Aspiring National Park.

INTRODUCING THE KEA

Kea are the only alpine parrot species in the world, but their population is under threat. There are now believed to be fewer than 5000 kea in the wild, which is why Ajax and I do the work we do. However, it's hard to estimate how many of them there are, as their habitat is so spread out across the South Island and much of it is in places that are pretty hard to access. Anyway, they're classified as being nationally endangered by DOC, which puts them into the second-highest threat category.

The reason they are considered under threat is that their range is restricted to the Southern Alps, and their population has been undergoing a rapid decline, which is predicted to continue. To put it into context, the kea are regarded as being as at risk as the yellow-eyed penguin, and more at risk than the great spotted kiwi, the banded dotterel and the whio or blue duck.

Given they can be pretty noisy, it seems appropriate that they got their name from the noise they make. They have a very particular call that sounds like they're saying 'keeee-aaaa'.

The Waitaha iwi, who were early residents of the South Island, believed that the kea were kaitiaki (guardians) of their people. When the first European settlers arrived, they didn't think there was any difference between kea and kākā, as they shared a lot of the same bush habitat, but in 1848 some Ngāi Tahu elders showed English naturalist Walter Mantell that the kea were, in fact, a distinct species. Mantell's findings were then presented to the Zoological Society of London in 1856, and the kea was given the scientific name *Nestor notabilis*. *Nestor* is the genus of both kea and kākā, and *notabilis* is Latin for 'noteworthy', which the kea certainly is.

They have mostly dull olive-green feathers, with a bit of black and blue, but when they fly you can see amazingly bright orange and red feathers under their wings, which have a span of up to a metre. There have been some reports of yellow or albino kea, but I've never seen one.

Their home in the Southern Alps of the South Island offers them a variety of habitats, including beech forests, alpine meadows and mountain scree slopes. It's an extremely harsh and varied environment, but kea are highly adaptable and can cope with change a lot better than most people do.

Kea nest on the ground, usually in rock cavities, but sometimes in hollow trees or among roots. They have a long nesting period— it takes around four months for chicks to fledge. Once fledged, the birds also have an extended juvenile phase, and are dependent on their parents for more than six months.

Kea are highly gregarious birds, and they form large, social flocks. The largest of these flocks tends to be made up of young males up to around three years old, while young females only seem to stay with their flocks during their first year. Once adult kea reach breeding age, at around three to four years old, they tend to leave the main flock, then pair up for breeding and raising chicks. They are monogamous and form long-term pair bonds.

It's not uncommon for birds to move between flocks, and this doesn't seem to cause any friction. The flocks don't seem to be based on any solid hierarchy or family system—they're a bit of a free-for-all. There's a good reason that a group of kea is known as a circus, as they can be pretty out there!

Kea love to get in people's faces. Go to a carpark around Arthur's Pass and they'll land on your car and start chewing on your windscreen wipers—or if you're at a ski field they'll be there trying to steal your lunch. They're super curious and will investigate anything new that they come across, which is why they're well known for destroying parts of cars and stealing trampers' bootlaces.

People don't associate birds that are so in-your-face with being endangered, but that's because a small number of them are highly visible in these environments. When you're studying them and looking for them in the mountains, they're not actually that abundant.

Kea live for about 30 years in the wild. The key to their survival is their ability to adapt quickly to their changing environment, and to exploit a variety of food sources. They're mostly vegetarian— eating most parts of plants, including fruit, flowers, seeds, roots and shoots—but they're opportunistic, and will eat pretty much anything. And when I say anything, I mean it: studies have shown them eating more than 200 varieties of natural food, including seabird chicks, insects and lizards. And that doesn't even include any of the human food that they'll happily snatch given half a chance.

Another day, another kea nest. This one's in Westland National Park. PHOTO BY ANA RICHARDS

An adult female kea in
Nelson Lakes National Park.

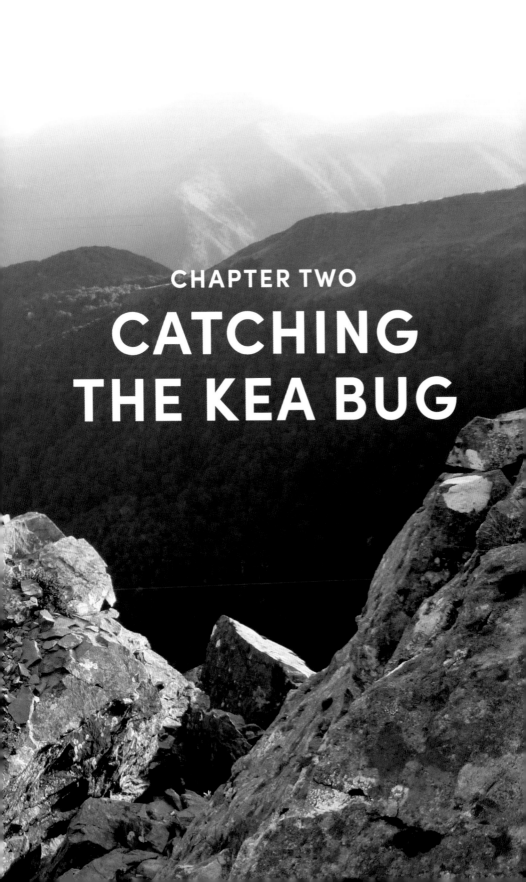

CHAPTER TWO
CATCHING THE KEA BUG

An adult male kea perches on a flax bush in Arthur's Pass Village.

After I got back from that first volunteer trip I kept working as a builder, but I started working long hours and saving up the extra time so I could get longer holidays. During my breaks, I'd go down to the South Island and do volunteer work for the Kea Conservation Trust. I was still a while off meeting Ajax for the first time, but I was getting closer to being certain that kea work was what I wanted to do. I just had to find a way to make it pay the bills.

It was worth doing my time, though, as through this work I made some good contacts and got to know the key people doing kea research. The best piece of advice I could give anyone who wants to work with wildlife or in conservation is to start by volunteering. Not only do you get great work experience, but it will also help you to decide whether it really is something you enjoy doing. If you want to volunteer, you need to be keen, and be even fitter than you are keen! You need to have some bush experience, and be able to turn your hand to whatever needs doing.

Gradually, I started going on trips where my expenses were being paid—I was still a volunteer but it wasn't costing me as much to go on the trips, which meant I could go more often. These trips usually involved a bunch of up to a dozen people, usually a mixture of people with kea experience and people completely new to the birds, heading out and surveying a set area for kea. We'd record any activity we saw and note potential nesting areas. We'd also catch and tag any unbanded birds and, in some cases, attach radio transmitters to them, so that we could track the birds' movements. Any birds that we caught would be measured and DNA samples collected to help us get a picture of the health and diversity of the population. Another job was to check transmitters in the area, and to track down any transmitters that were giving off a 'dead' signal. These signals are transmitted when the bird (or hopefully just the transmitter) hasn't moved for more than 12 hours.

It was challenging but really rewarding work. It meant being out in whatever conditions the South Island high country could throw at me—and then some. It could go from scorching hot to freezing cold and snowy within hours.

People thought I was a bit mad, spending all my hard-earned leave and overtime chasing around the mountainsides of the South Island in the middle of winter, but it gave me the chance to impress the crew from the Kea Conservation Trust. I began doing more volunteer work for them, starting with a couple of memorable trips to St Arnaud and the Nelson Lakes National Park in 2009.

There wasn't a job description for what I was doing, but if there had been I imagine it would have read something like this:

Wanted: Kea location scout/nest monitor

Mountain man or woman needed to leap around the hills of St Arnaud in search of kea nests. Must have 20/20 eyesight and be a kea-lover, able to traverse glacial rivers and happy to endure all manner of kea bites (affectionate or otherwise). Must not mind being wet for the majority of the day.

My job was firstly to find kea nests, and secondly to check if they were still being used. But finding kea nests isn't that straightforward. Then, if I managed to find a nest and no kea was home, I had to do a thorough check for signs of life—namely feathers, poo or kea nearby. For one of those things, the most accurate way for me to check was to do a good sniff test. Kea poo has a, shall we say, distinct aroma!

The reason I was looking for these nests was that I had been given the job of converting a 1990s paper map into an up-to-date GPS

A flock of juvenile kea at Death's Corner.

map that would provide a good snapshot of the kea population in the area, so their breeding success could be monitored. This meant spending a lot of time walking up and down mountains looking for obscure holes in the ground where kea might be nesting.

It was a bit like a treasure map. Reference points were provided and instructions were scribbled, but as I looked at the expansive, featureless rock-scape before me, the task seemed rather daunting. In order to reach certain nest sites, I had to cross some glacial, didymo-filled (read: slippery) rivers, which was best done in a pantless, bootless state. Then I would wander the hills like a mad man, poking my nose into any suspicious cavities. And—just like a madman—I would chuckle to myself when I thought about what my potential rescuers would think if anything went wrong and they found me in this scantily clad state frozen in a riverbed or clinging to a mountainside.

An historic, insulation-free DOC hut was my home for two rain-filled weeks. Its fire was my saviour. I set up my mattress next to it so I could stay warm during the night, and put extra logs on so it would still be going in the morning.

During my stay there, I eventually found a nest that had a bird inside, sitting on some eggs. Her mate was outside the nest, busy defending it from another male who had unknown intentions. This was the only nest I found with birds inside it. I found one more nest that looked like birds had been using it, and about 20 that were empty, with no sign of any life.

When I think back now on all that time I spent checking out holes that weren't kea nests and going down holes that had been used before but weren't being used any more, it makes me laugh. I'd stand there and look at them and think, *well, I reckon this has been used* . . . but there was no way of knowing whether it was reasonably fresh use or if it had been occupied the previous season.

Now, when I go up there with Ajax, I can get around those same nests way faster, as he can tell me exactly where the kea are or, at least, where they've been lately. That's especially the case if there is a cluster of nests that a bird has been using—he'll go straight to the one that it's in, whereas I used to have to check them all out.

As well as scouring rock-scapes, I went to more obvious spots to find kea—namely the cafeteria at the Rainbow Ski Area. Here, I successfully trapped an old male, and smuggled it back to my car to change its band, only to discover it had attached itself to my assistant's finger. I desperately looked around, trying to find a suitable alternative chew-toy, only to discover the best substitute was my thumb. Wounded and defeated, we finally made the decision to let this one roam free, in the hope that we might catch him next time around.

My next trip down to St Arnaud was early the following summer. On the first day out in the field I used the opportunity to check the ski field to see if there were any kea haunting the abandoned slopes, but it was void of kea as well as people. The only thing that was alive was the sky, which was busy hammering the area with rain. We left empty-handed.

Conscious of my monitoring goals, I visited a key site where a young kea family had been found nesting in August. Once again I was welcomed by a male kea sitting in a tree outside the nest, which was a good sign. After squeezing myself inside the rock cavity I was elated to see more than just the female kea running about the nook. There was mum and two chicks. The three eggs seen earlier had produced two living offspring—which is a great success rate in kea reproduction. This is when I realised that I would rather work with kea chicks than adults any day. They look just as cheeky, but they were so docile that I was able to catch them in my hands without any special trapping devices.

I caught one at a time and crawled out of the nest. I did the typical measurements, put some coloured bands on their legs and fitted radio transmitters on their backs. One thing that I found interesting was that these fledging kea were heavier than the typical adult. Both chicks were over 1 kilogram, and adults usually weigh a little less than that. It just shows how much effort must be involved in raising fledging chicks from eggs.

I might add, putting radio transmitters on parrots isn't an easy task. First you need to make the harness. You do this before you go out in the field, and it takes about 20 minutes from start to finish. The harness is designed to fall off after the battery in the transmitter has run out. There is no high-tech wizardry—rather, you just let wear and tear erode the cotton strings that lash the harness pieces together and then *voilà*—it falls off, kind of like taking off a cardigan.

During this trip, kea sightings in remote areas were so few and far between we decided to try our luck looking for birds at one of the huts nearby. Kea visit human habitation because often people can't resist feeding them; for them it's an easy way to get fed. We managed to convince someone at the local DOC office to give us a ride up the lake in their boat and made ourselves at home at the Coldwater Hut, at the southern end of Lake Rotoiti.

We yelled and whistled and waved around brightly coloured objects, hoping to attract kea. No birds were showing up, so I got engrossed in observing an interaction that is best described as eel versus duckling. The ducklings won.

Not long after this we were visited by a male kea, nicknamed Arnie, who we had caught at the ski field in August. He spent an hour or so amusing us and the trampers at the hut before flying off up the lake.

I took extra care to watch where he was going, in the hope of finding him and hopefully his nest the next day. It turned out that Arnie was nowhere close, however; there was no signal at all in any direction from his transmitter. So we spent the day walking back to St Arnaud in the rain.

The next day my brother arrived. He was a complete novice at kea hunting and this was my chance for revenge—after all those years of him picking on me when we were kids, a little kea punishment was in order! We spent two days searching for kea activity, but again we were left disappointed. I had high expectations that I would find eggs or chicks in a nest cavity we had spotted earlier, but alas it was empty.

It was a solemn walk down the mountain, because I had promised my brother that there would be some kea to see. We headed home to rest our aching bodies. After two days of this my brother was absolutely knackered and asked for a day off, so reluctantly I let him sit it out: I had pushed him hard enough. Maybe it was the rocks that I had hidden in his pack at the start of the trip that tired him out, or just the fact that he was unfit.

Since that first visit, I've been gone back up to those same nests every year to keep an eye on what's happening to the kea population in the St Arnaud area. The population there seems pretty stable, and while it's good that it hasn't decreased, it would be better to see it growing a little bit. Considering the amount of space there is up there, it's a bit surprising that there aren't more birds.

Back in Whanganui and back at work, I carried on hassling people for a job. Perseverance is a key attribute when it comes to doing this kind of work—both with the birds and with people. Eventually, it paid off. Or at least I thought it did. I got a job down at Mount Cook doing some kea research. I quit my building job, but about a week and a half before I was set to go down there I got an email from the researchers to say that their funding had been cut and there was no job for me. I was gutted. My boss in Whanganui said to me, 'Don't worry! You can just stay here and keep building.'

I thought about it for a bit then made my decision. *You know what? I've got a degree that I've spent all this time and money on, I'd better try to use it.* So that was the end of my building career and my time in Whanganui.

I went to Napier, where my girlfriend at the time lived, and started volunteering for DOC. I went out into the field with a guy called Rhys. I met him at the road end and he had his dog with him. I was a bit surprised to see it until I realised it was a trained kiwi dog. We headed out into the bush and it was absolutely awesome to see this dog tracking the birds so easily. I asked Rhys hundreds of questions about what his dog did, how he'd trained it and how he got into the Conservation Dogs Programme. I probably drove him nuts with all my questions, but he was really patient and told me all about it.

After that I did heaps of hunting with some other DOC workers who were controlling pigs in the area. They used dogs to indicate where the pigs were. Seeing how handy dogs could be in the field with Rhys was amazing, but seeing how these dogs worked as part of a team was a huge eye-opener. It was the first time I'd really had the chance to watch dogs work, while at the same time being able to look at them and know exactly what they were thinking. That was quite a revelation to me.

Eventually, this volunteering turned into a job with DOC. I spent a couple of summers in the Hawke's Bay chasing kiwi around and doing a bit of predator control—mostly we were trapping stoats and rats, as thankfully possums weren't too much of a problem there. It was good experience of being out in the elements, as I worked in quite mountainous parts of the region. The highest point was around 960 metres above sea level and it would snow occasionally.

It might sound a bit funny, but working with the pig dogs for a while made me realise that they do the same work as the bird dogs. Really, a kiwi dog is a dog hunting kiwi—just not killing them.

While I was working for DOC, one of my colleagues had a dog that she was training to find kiwi. She was going through all the tests to get her dog accredited to the DOC Conservation Dogs Programme. It was interesting to see the whole process that she had to go through with training and testing.

It was around that time that I seriously started thinking about getting a dog that I could work with. As well as being able to see the benefits of having a dog out in the field, I also reckoned that if my colleague's dog, which was pretty average, could pass then I'd probably be able to train a dog that could pass as well. Seeing the process at close quarters gave me the confidence that I'd be able to train a dog to do conservation work.

Eventually, after a while working in Napier then volunteering overseas during the winter when there wasn't any local DOC work for me—my overseas work included surveying Mexican spotted owl territories!—the call of the kea got too strong. I packed up and

My first paid kea trip in Mount Cook National Park.
I'm trying to pick up signals from any kea in the
area wearing transmitters. PHOTO BY FABRICE HIBERT

headed for the South Island, where I'd managed to get a job doing research for the Kea Conservation Trust.

While I was packing up to head south, there was one important job I had to do—find a new home for my pet pig. Percy was born in the wild; once while we were out hunting for work we'd killed his mum. We were collecting the pigs' heads for TB testing, and my workmate found him sucking on the dead, headless body. My workmate looked at me and said, 'You killed it. You've got to look after this one.'

I took the wee fella home, and within a day he thought I was his mum. I had him for almost a year. It was almost like having a little dog. He followed me around and he'd do what I told him. I'd take him for walks all the time—although as soon as he knew we were heading back home he'd take off and I'd have to chase him down the road. I'd tackle him and hang onto him as he was squealing and kicking. Then I'd have no choice but to carry him all the way home. That was my practice for having a dog!

Eventually I found him a new home, but then the guy who came to get him told me that he was planning on eating him. My then-girlfriend heard, and came flying out to tell him that that wouldn't be happening. She gave him all the food we had for Percy and told the guy exactly what to feed him and when. Weirdly, he agreed, and he took Percy home and his whole family fell in love with the pig. Percy was such a character that he saved his own life!

With Percy happily rehomed, I headed for the South Island. Because a lot of my work was in the Kahurangi National Park, in the northwest of the South Island, I based myself in Nelson, but I was a bit of a vagrant. I didn't have anywhere permanent to live, and I was up in the mountains so much I pretty much just lived out there and would sleep on the floor somewhere when I came into town. I lived in a caravan for a while, or would sleep on people's couches. My nana still lived in Christchurch, so sometimes I made myself at home there. I used to go to her place to do my washing, and she'd make me sandwiches. It was luxury for me.

The more I got involved with working with kea and the more I moved around the country doing conservation work, the more I saw other dogs working with birds. I met other conservation workers who had dogs, and I'd always talk to them about their training and the work that they did. All the time I was gaining knowledge and understanding of how the dogs worked and what it was like to have one to work with.

One guy who I became good mates with had a dog that was trained to work with kea, although he used it for other birds. That was what really got me thinking. Once I had myself a place to live, it was time to think about getting a dog—and not just any dog. I wanted a kea dog.

An adult female kea among the
southern rātā at Death's Corner.

A MISUNDERSTOOD BIRD

Human contact has affected kea in a number of ways. Māori used to take the birds for food (but they were found to be not very tasty and to have the nutritional value of a rock!) and for their colourful feathers. Until the arrival of the Māori, kea are thought to have been found more widely across the South Island, making their homes in the high-country areas of the Southern Alps.

When Europeans came to this country, there would have been an artificial population boom of kea, because they're really smart birds and they learn to exploit different sources of food really quickly. As the settlers came and brought sheep and other food sources, kea were able to exploit all of those things for their own benefit. They were one of the very few birds in New Zealand that benefited (in the short term) from the arrival of Europeans (one of the other ones being paradise ducks, because they love pasture). All the settlements that sprung up around the South Island meant there was plenty of food to be found by the birds, especially at dumps and on farms.

The kea's knack for exploring and exploiting has led them to discover new sources of food as their environment has changed. That's why they chew up windscreen wipers, people's packs and stuff like that. They're always learning and trying to find new food sources. Unlike most birds, kea aren't hard-wired to eat specific things, unlike their close relative the kākā. The kea has a massive memory for what's edible and where to find different food sources.

Eventually, the rise in the human population had two serious negative impacts on kea. The first was the clearance of forests and sub-alpine scrub and tussock land in order to make way for more farmland. The second and hardest hitting was the growing belief that kea were a threat to farm animals, and therefore needed to be controlled. This was largely because they were seen killing sheep. That definitely happened, but I'm pretty sure the number of sheep killed by the birds was greatly exaggerated. Farmers probably blamed greater losses on the birds than they actually suffered.

A lot of things needed to happen before kea started exploiting sheep as a food source. The sheep would need to be unshorn and unable to move for some reason—like being in a snow drift. While the sheep were stuck, the kea would come down and land in their fleece. They'd then get their beaks into the area of the sheep's back where the kidneys are. Once in there, the kea would dig out the energy-rich fat around the sheep's kidneys. This was a learned behaviour, and it only happened in certain areas. The sheep wouldn't die straight away, but instead would die gradually of blood poisoning. These days sheep can be inoculated against septicaemia, so if this happened now it wouldn't necessarily be fatal to the sheep. It still happens from time to time around Queenstown—it seems the birds down there have learned how to do it over the generations.

The first reports of kea killing sheep go back as early as 1867, near Wānaka. Not long after that, it became quite accepted for farmers to shoot and trap kea to protect their sheep. Bounties were put on the birds, and people got quite well paid to kill them.

But the real public battle against the birds was ramped up with the publication of a book by George Marriner called *The Kea: A New Zealand Problem* in 1908. It backed up the farmers' belief that these birds were a menace and should continue to be culled.

In a chapter called 'The Sheep Killer', Marriner makes it pretty clear what he thinks of the birds.

> The keas have several methods of attacking sheep, and it depends largely upon the kind of ground as to which one is used in a particular instance.
>
> They may attack in large numbers up to one hundred and twenty, or merely in ones and twos. Usually one or two old birds, known as 'sheep-killers', do the killing, and the others share the spoil.
>
> It is quite a mistake to suppose that all keas kill or even attack sheep. Just as we have comparatively harmless tigers, who will not attack a man except under provocation, and also 'man-eaters', who seem to take a special delight in killing men; so among the keas, many of them never

attack sheep, while others, usually old birds, seem to enjoy nothing better.

Marriner further goes on to prove how little he really understood these smart birds by saying that one reason they started attacking sheep was because they mistook them for 'woolly vegetable sheep'— actually a species of cushion plant, *Raoulia rubra*—that were home to large white grubs that the birds liked to eat.

There's a chapter of the book completely dedicated to repeating stories from shepherds and farmers who blamed the birds for multiple sheep casualties, particularly during snowy winters, when losses would have been high anyway.

The final chapter, 'Kea Hunting', is really disturbing, as it recounts the wholesale slaughter of the birds during the previous 40 years. At first, farmers and landowners funded hunters to shoot the birds in their thousands, then local councils started to offer a bounty for each kea beak. One farmer said: 'In my experience the damage done to the sheep has not been serious since a substantial reward was instituted. The payment of a high price for heads is the best means of keeping shepherds and others engaged in the hill country, continually on the war path.'

The kea bounties reached as much as £1 a beak (which is about $100 in today's money), leading to some farmers employing full-time kea hunters. They became really good at finding and killing the birds, even when they weren't providing any kind of threat to sheep. I've talked to some of the guys who used to do it, and they made a pretty good living out of it. Most of the professional guys would either shoot or poison the birds, but I've heard of some birds that were beaten to death with sticks. Records show that one hunter shot 400 kea over one winter season, with a horrifying 67 of them being killed in a single night.

Payments were made by the Department of Agriculture and the local authorities. From the records kept by the department, it's thought that around 150,000 kea were killed under this programme of slaughter in the 100 years until 1970, when they gained partial protection under the Wildlife Act and the bounties were finally withdrawn. That didn't stop the killing though, as farmers were still allowed to shoot kea if they believed them to be causing damage, for which the burden of proof was not very high. It was to be another 16 years before kea were given full protection under the Act.

The slaughter of the birds caused a population crash that mirrored the artificial boom they'd experienced with the arrival of Europeans. Unfortunately, the population crash was made much worse by the introduction of mammalian pests.

Of the introduced predators, stoats are the biggest threat to kea. They were introduced to the country in 1884, but it took them a long time to spread into kea habitat, having been released to counter the rabbit problem in the Mackenzie country. It also took them quite a while to reach saturation in the Southern Alps, but when they did, they hit the kea population hard.

One thing that has worked in favour of the kea is the fact that their breeding season starts early and lasts a relatively long time. Kea chicks born early in the season will fledge before the explosion in the stoat population that occurs in summer when young stoats become independent.

Interestingly, while still a risk, possums aren't as much of a threat to kea as they are to other native birds. Despite having been introduced earlier than stoats, they have spread much more slowly and only reached the high country of the South Island in the 1950s. The population density of possums also seems to decline with altitude, so they are yet to reach the kind of saturation that stoats have in these areas. Rats and cats are also an issue for kea, but much less so than stoats and possums. When rats are abundant, however, they'll steal eggs from the nests, which we've caught on camera.

With all of these things happening at the same time, the kea population tipped too far the wrong way, to the point that we're now left with only around 5000 birds in the wild. That's why I'm so dedicated to helping these birds to not only survive but to re-establish a more robust population.

A juvenile male kea gazes out from Death's Corner.

CHAPTER THREE

MEETING
AJAX

After spending so much time out in the mountains trying to seek out kea nests, it seemed obvious that a dog would make my job heaps easier. The dog could sniff out the kea before even seeing them, and so save me a lot of time.

Most people who train dogs for conservation work get certain breeds that are suited for the work, like Vizslas or German shorthaired pointers, which have a really strong point on them. (This means they indicate really clearly when they have found an item of interest.) I didn't have any really strong ideas about what breed I wanted. All I knew was that if I got a smart dog, I should be able to train it do whatever it needed to do.

Tamsin Orr-Walker, who was the co-founder of the Kea Conservation Trust, said to me, 'You should get a Catahoula.' She had some, and reckoned they were cool dogs to work with. I decided to find out about this unusual breed of dog.

Catahoulas are an American breed that sometimes get called Catahoula curs, Catahoula hog dogs or Catahoula leopard dogs, because some of them are spotted. They're named after a place in Louisiana, where they have been named the 'state dog'. They come in a range of colours, including red, blue, brindle, grey and black. It's quite common for them to have blue eyes but with darker sections in the iris, which is quite unusual.

One of the things that makes Catahoulas good for the type of work I wanted to do is the fact that they're renowned for being highly intelligent, and they have heaps of energy—both important things when you're planning on teaching a dog to find birds and on taking it out into the bush for long periods of time. They're supposed to be pretty even-tempered, which is important for a dog that's going to work with birds. They also have a good reputation as tracking dogs, but without the aggression that is sometimes associated with hunting dogs.

Near the end of 2011, Tamsin sent me a link to a TradeMe listing. It turns out that she'd set up an alert for any listings that mentioned Catahoulas, so she'd know if anyone was selling them. This listing was for some Catahoula-cross puppies that were free to a good home. The only catch was that the dogs were in Westport. However, I rang the people who were giving the dogs away, and they told me that there were a couple of pups left in the litter.

I had a flat in Nelson by this stage, so me and my flatmate hopped in the car and headed across to the coast one rainy weekend. It was about a three-hour drive. I decided I wanted a male dog, and I already had a name picked out. In fact, I'd decided on the name long before I'd even really thought seriously about getting a dog. He was going to be called Ajax, after the warrior in Greek mythology who led the Greek soldiers in the Trojan War.

When we got to Westport, the owners took us out to see the puppies. Their mum was a border collie and their dad was a Catahoula, possibly with a bit of Labrador in him. There was a whole litter of them there, and they were all pretty cute.

I went through a bit of a process to decide which one I wanted. It went something like this: 'I'll have that one.' 'Oh, no, sorry mate, that one's taken.' 'What about that one?' 'That one's taken too.' 'Ummm, OK, what about that one?' 'Taken.' 'Right, so, what about him?' 'Yep, he's available.'

I had a look at what turned out to be the last available male pup. Thank goodness I did, as that one was Ajax, and that moment ended up being a real turning point in the way I would approach working with kea. He didn't look anything like a Catahoula, but I hoped he'd have some of the traits the breed were renowned for.

My flatmate had stood and watched the whole performance. She then pointed to one of the other dogs. 'What about that one?'

'Yep, that one's still available.'

'Right,' she said. 'I'll take that one, too!'

She'd never even talked about wanting a dog, but we ended up with not one but two puppies to take back to Nelson.

That trip was an experience in itself. We put the two pups, each a bit over two months old, into a box and put it on the back seat of the car. The pair of them got a bit bored quite early on in the trip and set about destroying the box. They ended up just hanging out on the back seat together.

That would have been fine, as they were so small, except we hadn't really thought about the fact that neither of them were house-trained, so they just pissed and shat everywhere. The back seat of my car was an absolute filthy, stinking mess. It was covered in poo, which the puppies then happily rolled in, meaning there was poo all over them as well. There was shit smeared into all the cracks in the back seat, and they tried to get into front seat to visit us, so there was a bit on the sides of the front seats as well. It was carnage back there—and it didn't smell too good from up the front either.

If that wasn't bad enough, the windy road through the Buller Gorge made Ajax car-sick. So along with all the poo and wee, he added a good amount of spew to the mix.

We stopped at a rest area about halfway back home and did our best to have a bit of a clean-up of the back seat with some wet-wipes I had in the car, but they didn't really help much. We just had to put up with the mess and the smell until we got home.

That was only the start of things. Having two small puppies at home was absolute chaos. Most of the time they were pretty cool little dogs, but there were times when I was glad I hadn't paid anything for the little brats, as I would have wanted my money back!

One of the worst times was actually my own fault. A few weeks after we got the dogs, I went out to feed them. I had an open can of dog food in my hand, and as I was scooping the food out for them, both puppies came flying in and knocked the can out of my hand. I bent down to grab it and the half-open lid was facing up. The lid of the can sliced straight into my hand—I had a big flap of skin

Ajax (left) with his sister, Molly, when they were puppies. PHOTO BY KIRSTY JONES

Even as a puppy, Ajax was a keen swimmer. PHOTO BY KIRSTY JONES

Ajax as a puppy, exploring
Rabbit Island in Nelson.

hanging off my palm. I was covered in blood and dog food. It was gross. I managed to stick the skin back on and cleaned the whole thing out with disinfectant.

The next day I went into work and asked my boss whether he thought I needed stitches. One look at the wound and he went a bit of a weird colour and said, 'YES!' I reckoned it looked like it was gelling back together though, so I decided to give it a few days. I didn't end up getting stitches and it came right eventually. It cracks me up that people think the work I do is pretty dangerous but I managed to injure myself that badly just feeding the dog at home.

In those early days, Ajax was a shy but excitable little dog. I quickly realised that he loved getting attention. When people greeted him with scratches and head pats, he would wiggle his entire body so much that he'd end up whipping himself with the tip of his own tail. But then he developed another less appealing trick.

He was such a cute puppy that people would always want to pat him. He'd get really wiggly and super excited at getting so much attention—so excited, in fact, that he'd lose control of his bladder and start pissing everywhere. It happened so many times. There'd be people patting him and going on about how gorgeous he was—and he'd be standing there, wiggling happily and pissing on their feet. Thankfully, no one ever seemed to notice—they were so distracted by his puppy-dog eyes that they would be completely unaware of what he was up to. They would wander off carrying a slightly acrid aroma around with them for the rest of the day. The odd time he'd pee so much that I'd have to point it out to people. That was always kind of embarrassing. 'I'm glad you like my dog. He's pissing on your shoes.' It took him a while to grow out of that, but I was really glad when he did.

One of the naughtiest things he did when he was a puppy was one time when I left him with some friends. They were going out, so they put Ajax in the bathroom because they were worried about him causing chaos in the house. While they were gone, Ajax chewed up

Ajax poses with our friend Pietro Sandini at Rabbit Island in Nelson.

half the bathroom floor instead. They didn't tell me about it for ages because they were scared of getting this cute wee puppy in trouble. When they finally confessed to me I said, 'You should have told me!', but they said, 'Oh na, we were getting a new bathroom anyway, so it didn't really matter.'

While I was now the proud owner of a new puppy, there were quite a few challenges ahead of us. There were times when it seemed like it might have been easier to train a kea. As well as being incredibly funny, kea are considered to be one of the most intelligent bird species in the world, while there were very few signs that Ajax was smart at all. I knew from the start that it was going to be a long process if I was ever going to turn him into a crack kea-locating dog.

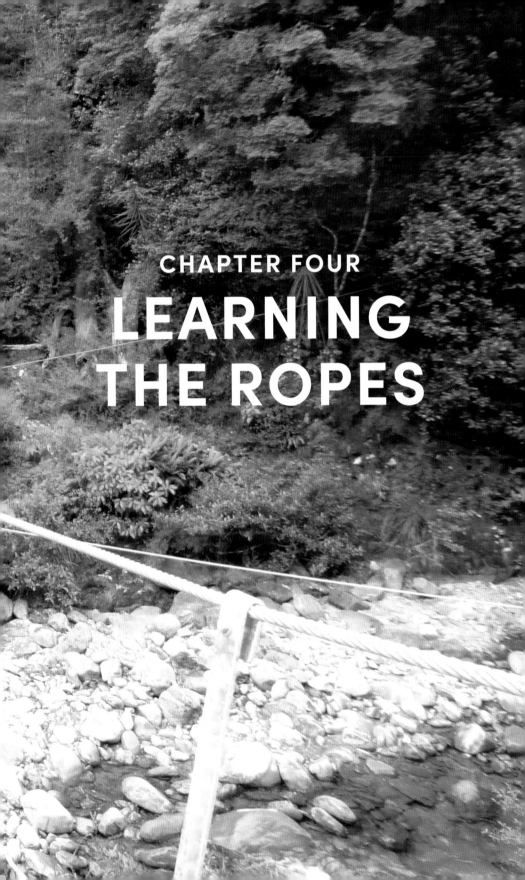

CHAPTER FOUR

LEARNING THE ROPES

Pretty much as soon as I got him home, I started training Ajax. He's super chilled out and really well behaved now, but back then he was a bit of a handful. Like most puppies, he had his own ideas about things and they were sometimes a bit different to mine.

Back then he was an outdoor dog, and he pretty much lived in the back yard the whole time. That made toilet-training him pretty easy. After the poo-sloshing trip back from Westport in the car and the shoe-peeing incidents, this was a very good thing. I reckon it's really important for anyone who gets a dog to start training them straight away, unless they want the dog to be really annoying.

Speaking of annoying, Ajax did manage to wind me up a couple of times when he was a puppy. One night after work, I took him for a walk around the streets in Richmond where we lived at the time. I guess I'd taken him a bit further than our usual walks had been, but it wasn't that far. Anyway, Ajax decided that he'd had enough of this walking business, so he just sat down in the middle of the footpath. Talk about stubborn! No matter what I tried, he absolutely refused to move his legs. I pulled on his lead. I nudged his bum with my foot. I growled at him. I asked him nicely. Nothing worked. In the end, after a few minutes of cajoling, there was nothing for it but to pick him up and carry him home.

As well as sharing the garden with his sibling, Ajax had some native geckos as neighbours. Well, I say 'neighbours' because they lived in an enclosure that I'd built for them in the garden. They were pretty rare lizards, and I could only have them as pets because

I'd been given them by a registered breeder and I had a permit to keep them. Clearly Ajax didn't have any idea just how precious his cold-blooded neighbours were—I reckon he just found them pretty intriguing entertainment.

One day, I got home from work and Ajax came out to meet me. Compared to his usual bat-out-of-hell run when he heard my truck arrive, this day he wandered out quite slowly, and he looked really guilty. I wondered straight away what he'd done, but he just skulked off into the garden.

Ajax went on acting a bit weird, staying away from me while I was doing all my usual after-work stuff. I didn't really think much more about it, until a bit later when I went out to feed the lizards.

The first thing I noticed was that the plants that had been in their enclosure had all been turfed out. What the hell? Then I noticed that on the side of one of the enclosures there was a big hole in the fly mesh. It all started to make sense.

Ajax's curiosity had obviously got the better of him. He'd rammed his head in through the mesh and ruined the enclosure. Maybe he'd got his face stuck and ended up pulling out the plants while he was trying to extricate himself from what he clearly had worked out was not an ideal situation—I'll never know exactly how it played out, but I know him well enough to know that he would have felt terrible about being so naughty, especially knowing that he'd definitely get caught.

But the news for my super-curious dog was about to get much worse—one of the geckos had escaped.

'AJAAAAAAAXXXX!' I roared. He slunk towards me from the corner of the garden, the look on his face a cross between guilt and fear. He knew he'd done something really bad, but that didn't stop me from reinforcing that in no uncertain terms. He just sat there, taking the biggest telling-off of his life. In fact, he was getting such a good telling-off that one of our neighbours popped her head over the fence to ask if everything was OK! I think she was only slightly less shocked than Ajax was at my being so mad at him.

I'd always known that one of the important things about training a dog is that you have to show them who's boss, but I wasn't expecting it to happen that particular day. But after that, Ajax definitely understood the pecking order in our house. He might have been a super-cute fluffball of a puppy, but he was still quite closely related to wolves and other pack animals, and as such he needed an alpha dog to look to. After that incident, he was in no doubt that I was the boss.

The gecko incident was soon overshadowed by another visitor to our property to whom Ajax had a completely different reaction. He was only a few months old when a hedgehog wandered into our back yard one evening. Given I had been thinking about training Ajax to become a wildlife conservation dog, I realised this would be a good test of how he was going to react to another species turning up in his realm.

My flatmate's dog was also there, barking at this tiny, spindly mammal that was curled up in a corner of the yard. Ajax? Well, he was cowering in the corner, trying to work out what the hell this prickly ball thing was. There was no fearsome standing of ground or inquisitive sniffing at the prickly beast.

Eventually the hedgehog unfurled itself and sauntered away without so much as a nip or sniff from Ajax. With the intruder gone, Ajax slowly recovered from his terrifying encounter with this hideous predator by retreating to the safety of his kennel to have a good think about what had happened. I got to thinking, too—about whether I'd chosen the wrong dog.

It wasn't a good sign. But I quickly came up with a possible solution (just don't tell Ajax about this). I asked my flatmate if she wanted to swap dogs. Terrible, I know. But she didn't have to think for very long before she came back with a pretty strong 'Nah'.

I'd talked to other people with work dogs about what to look for. They'd pretty much all said that the dogs need to be quite feisty. This thing I had was not remotely feisty in the face of such a small thing as a hedgehog, so I wondered how on earth he would cope with larger creatures. If he was scared of a hedgehog, how would he ever deal with a curious, in-your-face kea? Would I ever be able to turn him into a kea-finding, mountaineering dog that would, like me, spend most of his time in the Southern Alps scouring the forests that blanket the valley sides, looking for kea nests?

I figured that there was really only one way to find out. Besides which, I had him (or he had me, I'm not sure which) now, so I decided I'd do my best to train him anyway.

In order to be allowed to take Ajax out kea-finding with me, he had to be accepted into the Conservation Dogs Programme and become registered. Even though I was doing most of my work for the Kea Conservation Trust, Ajax had to go through the DOC certification and become part of its programme. I needed to do this because I wanted to work with him in national parks, and any dogs that work there have to be certified by DOC.

Certain breeds of dog aren't allowed at all in the programme—breeds like kelpies and pit bulls, the kinds of dogs that are unpredictable or impractical to have in the bush.

Getting onto the DOC programme required ticking a lot of things off a list. First, before I could even get him on the programme, I had to prove there was the work available to make it necessary to have a dog trained in kea tracking. That wasn't difficult. Then I had to answer some quite tough questions about what I would do if my dog failed the programme. That was more difficult, but I thought that was good, because it meant that they were looking out for Ajax's welfare on the off-chance he didn't make it through the testing process.

Of course, Ajax wasn't much use in helping me with all the paperwork I had to do on his behalf, but he did come into his own when it came to the actual training. In order to get onto the programme, Ajax had to be able to perform an elaborate set of behaviours perfectly.

Obedience is a major factor in determining whether or not a dog passes the test, so I had to train Ajax to come when I called him, stop and stay on command, walk at heel, walk on a lead and, most importantly, avoid non-target animals. (I knew that last one wouldn't be a problem if they decided to test him on hedgehogs!) I also had to be able to prove that I was in control of Ajax at all times.

Once I'd sussed out exactly what the DOC people would want to see Ajax do, I had to make sure that these behaviours formed the foundation of what we worked on every day. To be honest, I probably had to learn as much as Ajax did when it came to the training. I'd never trained a dog before, so while he was trying to work out what I wanted him to do, I was trying to work out how to get him to do what I wanted!

I soon realised that consistency was really important for both Ajax and me when it came to training. And I found that Ajax was a pretty quick learner, as long as we repeated things regularly.

When I got home from work each day, Ajax would be there waiting for me, keen to get out and have some work-related fun at the park close to where we lived. We'd just play with a ball to start with. Eventually, I taught Ajax to bring the ball back to me. When he did what I wanted, I'd give him a wee food reward that I'd have hidden in my pockets.

Sometimes it was me who got a bit of training from Ajax, and it took him a while to teach me that he wasn't that interested in being given food for doing what I wanted. Eventually I worked out that what he really loved was when I'd give him a good pat and say 'Good booooooy!' When I did that, he'd be absolutely amping to get back to work and learn something else. This was a great discovery for me, as it meant that I didn't have to worry about accidentally putting pockets full of dog biscuits through the wash, and it also meant that Ajax could keep learning new stuff even when I didn't have any treats for him.

It's pretty unusual to have a dog that's not food-fixated, but Ajax really couldn't care less about getting treats—he'd much rather have a bit of positive feedback and a good pat. He just loves gaining people's approval and a bit of affection.

The other benefit of this was that it was much easier to teach Ajax that I was in charge by being kind to him rather than by shouting or growling at him. Also, unlike a lot of other dogs, it means he's never tried to sneak food or scavenge it. That's good because it means he's not at risk in areas where there's edible pest control, like rat poison.

Once he'd got the hang of bringing me back a ball, we started with some other basic things like getting him to sit on command. I'd stand next to him, say 'Sit, Ajax, sit!' and gently push him down. If he sat down, I'd give him heaps of praise. Then when I wanted him to lie right down, I'd say 'Down, Ajax, down!' and push his shoulders down a wee bit. It didn't take long for him to associate what I wanted him to do with the words and the fact that he'd get loads of praise once he did what I wanted.

When I started training him to heel, I'd put him on the lead and say 'Here!', then bring him in next to me. Once I could tell that when he heard me say 'Here!' he knew he needed to be next to me, then I would go further away from him and say it and he'd come straight for me. It was impressive how quickly he worked stuff out for himself. He sussed out 'sit', 'lie down', 'stay' and 'come here' pretty easily, but getting him to do things that didn't involve being right next to me was a bit trickier.

If he wasn't on the lead and I wanted him to stop, I didn't want him to be right beside me. It took me a while to work out how to get him to do this. I would tell him to stay, walk away a bit and put some food down, then keep walking. When he walked up to check out the food, I'd say 'Stop!', and he realised that I wanted him to stay still.

A lot of training Ajax was about the tone of voice I used. Dogs are very keyed in to tone, so if I called out 'Stop!' really sharply, Ajax quickly sussed out that I wanted him to make a sharp stop.

Sometimes when we were training I'd wait for him to do things naturally, then let him know that that was what I wanted him to do. Then I'd give him the command and he'd start figuring out the connection when he got that positive reinforcement.

Once he'd learned one skill, he would be looking for the next thing. He was all about trying to please me and trying to anticipate what I wanted him to do. When he looked at me, I could tell he was wondering what I wanted him to do next.

It wasn't long before he had all the usual commands—'sit', 'stay', 'come here', 'fetch', 'lie down', 'roll over' and that sort of stuff—absolutely in the bag. Sometimes I almost felt like he was looking at me and thinking, *really? That again? When are we going to get to the hard stuff?* He just loved learning new skills and tricks, partly because he'd get heaps of praise and partly because he's just a really brainy dog.

There was one thing that did worry me a bit when I first starting taking Ajax to the park. I had no idea how he'd get on with other dogs. Sometimes the most relaxed dogs can get a bit territorial. But I needn't have worried at all. Other dogs would cruise over to suss him out and he'd sit there and let them. It was almost crazy how chilled out he was, and that lack of interest meant the other dogs would eventually just wander off. Well, except for the odd time that dominant male dogs would start humping him. He would stand there with no idea what was going on!

He was the same with aggressive dogs. When other dogs bark at him heaps or get up in his face, he looks at them as if to say, 'Whatever, man, just chill out!' He's so cruisy that he doesn't respond, he just sits there looking a bit confused. It probably works in his favour, as it confuses the hell out of the other dogs as well!

The training didn't end at the park. Back at home there was plenty for Ajax to learn. Because he spent most of his time outdoors, he was always happy to be hanging out inside with me, even if it did mean doing some work.

One of the first things I got him to do at home was bring me my slippers. This took him about 15 minutes to work out. I'd show him the slippers, then go and put them in another room and ask him to go and find them. He'd shoot off out of the room, tail wagging, and be back in seconds with them in his mouth.

Then I'd hide each slipper in different places in the house. He'd bring me one, and I'd tell him to go find the other one. That took him about five minutes to work out. Once he'd nailed the whole slipper thing, it was onto my socks, then my shoes, then my boots, then my jandals.

The amazing thing was that he very quickly worked out which

shoes I was talking about, and he'd go and get exactly the right piece of footwear. He surprised me continuously with feats of what seemed to be human language comprehension as well as an uncanny ability to predict what I would do next.

There was one little glitch, though. If there was nothing much happening around the house, we hadn't been to the park and he was getting a bit bored, Ajax would go off, collect some of my socks and bring them to me as a way to get attention. It was hard for me not to laugh, seeing him wander in with a pair of socks hanging out of his mouth, looking very pleased with himself. He always seemed a bit surprised not to get a big pat and a 'Good boy!' out of it.

Once he'd worked out what all my different types of footwear were called and looked like, we branched out. Ajax learned to bring me my keys, my wallet and my phone. It was almost like having a canine butler—if I was leaving the house, Ajax was really good at making sure I had everything I needed to take with me. He was always happy to bring the wallet and the phone, but he really didn't like picking up the keys. It's possibly because of the noise they made, or maybe he didn't like the feel of them on his mouth—but knowing Ajax, it was probably because he suspected that I was going to drive off and leave him at home by himself.

When we were doing all the initial training, Ajax and I were always close together. To make it a bit more challenging for him, I slowly started moving further and further away when I was telling him to stop or stay. Eventually, it got to a point where I'd be so far away that Ajax couldn't hear me telling him what I wanted him to do. I'd yell and he would just be sitting there looking at me, a bit confused. He could tell that I wanted something, but he couldn't work out what.

This was one of those times when I was on as steep a learning curve as Ajax was. I decided to test something out and see if I could teach him some hand signals. He picked them up really quickly, and they have turned out to be super useful out in the bush, so long as Ajax can see me. He'll sit there with eyes fixed on me and when I give him a signal to 'sit', 'stay', 'come here' or 'move forward', he'll react really quickly and do exactly what I want. It's great when we're somewhere that's quite noisy—like by a river or on a hillside in high winds. The other time hand signals are really handy is if we come across birds or predators which I don't want to be startled by me whistling or shouting at the dog.

When we're walking along, if I want him in front, there's a command for that. His favourite command, though, is 'slow down', because then he knows there's something going on that he's going to be able to get amongst.

He knows 'wait', which is kind of informal and it tells him to hold up until I get there, then he can get going again. 'Stay' is much more formal, and he knows not to move no matter what. It's really handy in the bush. We often practise it as we walk along out in the forest, just to keep him fresh.

Once he'd had all the usual dog obedience training that your average domestic dog gets, as well as the other list of stuff that DOC expected from him, it was time for Ajax to be introduced to the great outdoors beyond the neighbourhood park. After all, if he was going to be a kea dog, he needed to be able to hang with me in the mountains.

To start with, we'd go to places in the forest where any dogs are allowed. While you can't take dogs into the national parks, there are quite a few forest parks and conservation areas under DOC control in the Nelson/Marlborough area where you can take a dog as long as you have a permit. One of the big ones is the Mount Richmond Forest Park, which covers 160,000 hectares of land between Nelson and Blenheim. It includes the Richmond Range, and a number of big rivers flow through it, including the Wairau, Pelorus and Waimea. It was a great place to take Ajax to get him used to being out in the bush. The landscape was pretty much identical to what Ajax and I would be working in if and when we got to work in the nearby Kahurangi National Park.

One other place I used to take him was the Raglan Range, which

Ajax out and about in northwest Nelson.

is part of a DOC area up by St Arnaud. The range was pretty close to where I lived, so I could easily take Ajax out there on the weekends. The open beech forest made it a really good place to go to practise climbing, crossing streams and doing all the bush stuff that a kea dog would have to do as part of his daily work, all except looking for the actual birds. That didn't come until quite a bit later.

It took me a while to get used to having Ajax with me in the bush. I was so used to heading off at my own pace to do what I needed to get done. Having a dog along with me, especially one that was still quite young and small, with short little legs, meant I had to learn to slow down a wee bit. Ajax did his best to keep up and stay alongside me, but sometimes I'd just be going too fast or he'd get a little bit involved in discovering this big new world he was encountering for the first time. There was so much to sniff and see and explore that sometimes I'd be walking along and he'd get left behind.

I figured that if I kept walking, he'd work out that he had to stick with me. It didn't quite work that way, because I'd forgotten that it was all new and exciting for him. Knowing Ajax, he would have been quite conflicted between wanting to hang out with me and wanting to find out what all these new smells were. Usually, the new smells would win out and he'd end up getting further and further behind.

Once his curiosity about whatever had grabbed his attention had been satisfied, he'd suddenly come back to reality and realise that I wasn't standing there beside him. And when Ajax noticed I wasn't there, he would freak out and start whining. And when he whines, everyone knows about it. He sounds like he's in really terrible pain.

The first few times I heard him do it, I panicked that something had happened to him and ran back to find him. He'd see me coming, stop crying, wag his tail furiously and race towards me, happy to be reunited. Put yourself in his shoes (paws): you're in this massive new environment that's far away from home, full of sights, sounds and smells that are foreign to you, and you only know one person. And they've just disappeared. You'd feel pretty freaked out, too, I reckon.

Once I worked out that he wasn't injured but was worried about me abandoning him, I slowed down so he could keep up with me while he got used to his new surroundings. Eventually, the novelty wore off a bit for him and he worked out that he could keep up with me—and sometimes even get way ahead of me, when he was feeling really energetic.

No matter where I worked with Ajax while I was training him, if we were out in the bush he'd always have a muzzle on, to ensure that he couldn't bite or eat anything he wasn't supposed to. I think it would be fair to say that he absolutely hated wearing it. He's not alone in that. Every dog I've ever seen having a muzzle put on hates it.

He'd make a bit of a fuss every time I put it on him. He'd wriggle around and rub his face on things, trying to get it off. But once we got going he'd forget about it, as he had plenty of sounds and smells to distract him. By the time he was on the move, it didn't seem to bother him too much.

It didn't take long, though, before I realised I'd made a rookie mistake by buying him a plastic muzzle. One day we were out walking and we stopped to have some lunch and a bit of a drink. I loosened Ajax's muzzle so that he could eat and drink comfortably. (He can drink with the muzzle on, but it's quicker for him if I take it off.) This day, it was off his face but still dangling around his neck, so I could put it back on once he'd eaten and had a drink.

While I was sitting having my lunch I noticed a sound I hadn't heard Ajax make before. It was a crunching sound, which I thought was a bit weird as I'd only given him dog roll for his lunch. I looked over to see him chomping on his muzzle. In a matter of seconds he'd chewed off the front of it and the thing was lying in pieces on the ground. It was completely wrecked but he looked quite pleased with himself. Needless to say the replacement one was made of steel!

Once Ajax was used to being out in the bush and he'd worked out that he needed to keep up with me, it was time to introduce him to some work-related experiences. I still wasn't allowed to take him out in the national parks, but I figured that one way he could have some experience of the type of work we would be doing was to take him out tramping with me.

On one of our tramping trips, Ajax surprised me by showing me some innate skills that, up until that point, I hadn't realised he had. After the hedgehog incident, I still wasn't sure if he had what it took to be a good bird dog, but on this particular trip he really impressed me and completely changed my mind.

We were walking along in the forest at the end of the Wangapeka Track, which is part of Kahurangi National Park. It's one of the few places in the park where you can take a dog, but only if you have a hunting permit and a permit for your dog, and even then you can't stay overnight. As long as the right paperwork is done and you stick to the permitted areas, DOC actually encourages people to hunt and kill red deer and pigs in the park.

The Wangapeka Track crosses from near Karamea on the West Coast right across to the Waimea Basin in the east, crossing two high saddles and following the beech-lined valleys of the Wangapeka, Karamea and Taipo rivers along the way. As well as providing a superb tramping track for people, the trail also provides an easy pathway for pigs to get around the park.

This particular day, we were near the eastern end of the track. It almost felt a bit dishonest when I got a permit for him as a pig-hunting dog, as he'd never shown the slightest inclination to hunt anything. Still, it was a good chance for him to get out into the bush with me, and I thought maybe he'd learn a thing or two along the way.

As we were walking across a flat spot close to the river, a little pig ran across our path. Quick as anything, Ajax was onto it. He took off after the piglet, stayed right on its curly tail and eventually got it bailed up next to a river. When I managed to catch up with him, Ajax had the creature trapped against the riverbank at an angle that meant the pig couldn't get away. He was standing there, completely on alert, barking at the piglet but not touching it at all. It was brilliant to see how perfectly he rounded up the pig without hurting it. He just got it where he wanted it and waited for me to come and find him. Seeing him do that made it really clear to me that he had good instincts when it came to tracking and trapping.

When I got there, I moved in while he kept the pig bailed up. He

Ajax stands guard over a pig in Kahurangi National Park. This was the day he started showing potential as a tracker.

clearly knew that I was going to come and do something with the pig, so he kept it there while he waited for me to move in.

While Ajax watched on, I got my little pocketknife out of my pack and stuck the pig. Once it was dead, I chopped off some meat to give to Ajax as a reward for his work. But he wouldn't eat it! He was much more enthusiastic about all the pats and praise that I gave him for doing such a good job.

Since then, he's made it abundantly clear to me that he hates pork. He won't touch it at all—no matter if it's cooked or fresh. Before I realised how much he hated the meat, I tried to shove it in his mouth a couple of times, but each time he'd spit it out and look at me, slightly disgusted. He's always quite happy to have a feed of goat when I get one of them, but pig? No way.

Up until he got that pig, Ajax hadn't really shown any natural instinct for tracking—all he'd managed to do was prove that he was a nice dog, which made him absolutely great to be around but not all that useful for work. But his behaviour when he got that pig was so natural, it made me realise that he had a chance at becoming a good working dog.

Once he was used to the bush environment, Ajax soon started to learn a few skills that your average town dog never needs to know. Before long, he had mastered swimming across rivers, scrambling up rocks, traipsing through snow drifts and sticking his nose down holes.

With the rivers and the rocks, we started small and built our way up. To start with, I'd walk Ajax through creeks and get him to follow me up over quite little rocks. When I saw that he was good at those things I'd increase the tempo a bit. I'd take him on bigger adventures, get him to go through deeper rivers where he'd have to swim rather than walk across, and I'd get him onto rocks that he'd have to scramble up rather than step over. He took to it all like a complete natural.

The first time I took Ajax out in the snow, I took him up Mount Fyffe out the back of Kaikōura. At just over 1600 metres high, it's a reasonable climb. In summer the mountain is usually bare but it's pretty much always covered in snow in winter.

I had no idea what to expect of Ajax's first encounter with snow. I was really worried about his feet being too cold, and that he'd get scratches on his paws from the ice. It sounds a bit silly now, but at the time I just didn't know how he would cope.

As we climbed higher up the mountain, Ajax didn't let up his speed. He stuck with me the whole way. Eventually, we walked onto the snow and I watched him to see how he'd react. Was he going to freak out? Was he going to look at me as if to say, 'Why have you brought me here?' Was he going to sit down at the edge of it and refuse to go any further? Yeah, it turned out I was worrying for no reason. He kept on walking as if nothing had even changed and he hadn't even noticed the white stuff underfoot. He was completely unfazed by the experience and just kept on going.

At the end of the day, I was still a bit worried about whether he was OK, so I checked his feet—they were absolutely fine. He was a complete natural. It was pretty much the same with every other type of terrain I took him onto. Wherever I went, he would follow, and if it was good enough for me, then it was good enough for him.

There was one thing he never quite learned to do and that's walking across a three-wired bridge. To be fair, dogs aren't really designed to cross what is effectively a tightrope with two higher wires to hang onto. To get across these basic bridges, I used to carry him around my neck in a fireman-type hold. I could tell he felt really secure when I carried him around my neck, and that helped to convince him that I was a trustworthy teammate. As he got bigger, it was a bit harder to sling him around my neck, but he's always happy to be handled and carried when he needs to be.

The more time we spent out in the wild together, the more Ajax became used to the terrain and the challenges that we encountered out there. Since then, he's become a really intrepid adventure dog, and we've had some pretty amazing exploits together outside of work, too. Ajax has done a heap of stuff most people never get to do—think rock climbing, abseiling, canyoning, boating, caving, camping and tramping.

Ajax with his first muzzle in the Wairau Valley.

As a vital part of his training, Ajax also started learning about kea. I had a wing feather from a kea, so I put it up on the wall at home. I'd say, 'Where's the kea?', and he'd go up and point to the feather. He knew exactly what I was asking him to find.

If we were ever at someone else's house, I'd ask him where the kea was and he'd always start looking up on the wall, trying to find the kea feather that I had at home. I knew then that he hadn't quite worked out that it was the actual feather I wanted, and that he still related that question, 'Where's the kea?', with the space on the wall. Clearly we still had a bit of work to do.

Eventually, Ajax sussed out that it was the bird feather that I was asking him to find. Once he'd got that worked out, I started him on more kea feathers—I made a pillow out of some feathers that I'd got from a dead kea. I'd hide the pillow around the house and I'd get him to sniff that out before I fed him. I'd say, 'Where's the kea?', and he'd take off and find the pillow. When he brought it back, I'd give him a big pat and then feed him.

Ajax is so good at sniffing things out, he would probably be able to find anything that was alive with a bit of practice. But he was particularly tuned in to the attention that I'd give him when he found the thing that I wanted. When he found kea-related things, I'd give him lots of pats and hugs. If he went after something I didn't want him to touch, I'd give him a loud, grumpy 'Leave it!', and he soon learned to leave those things alone. The more I praise him for doing something good, the better he gets at it.

Eventually, I started training him to be around other birds, like ducks. He was happy as. He learned quickly that they were nothing to be interested in and he never really bothered chasing them.

Once I was staying at a friend's house in Auckland, and had Ajax with me. My friend's neighbour had chickens that were free-range, and they popped over the fence. Ajax was out the back, and I watched him sprint up to these chickens. I thought, *this is the test that he needs*, and sat back to watch what he'd do.

He ran up to them and then just stood there and looked at them. The chickens weren't scared of him—they kept doing what they

Ajax, unfazed by the snow in Kahurangi National Park.

were doing and didn't run away. Because they didn't care, Ajax just sat and watched them. This was without any bird-aversion training. He was interested in them and seemed to know that he could watch them and let me know that they were there, but he also knew not to touch them.

I was pretty impressed. It was time for him to take the test to see if he was good enough to become a working dog.

THE CONSERVATION DOGS PROGRAMME

While training Ajax to be a kea dog was a new thing in the early 2010s, there's quite a long history of people working with dogs in conservation in New Zealand. There have been plenty of other amazing dogs doing some cool stuff for conservation here.

Dogs can be trained to seek anything that has a smell. There are now even dogs that have been trained to sniff out certain types of cancer, and some that can find antibiotic-resistant bacteria in hospitals. In New Zealand, some are trained to detect things as specific as kauri dieback disease. That's pretty amazing.

It's all down to the fact that a dog's sense of smell is more than 10,000 times more powerful than a human's. They have 50 times as many olfactory receptors as we do, so they can smell things more acutely, tell the difference between smells really easily, and are able to pinpoint the source of a smell way more accurately.

Here in New Zealand, DOC has a programme where dogs are trained to hunt different species of birds, mammals, reptiles and even plants. The department has been using dogs for conservation work for more than 40 years, but the use of dogs to help protect native species in this country goes all the way back to the 1890s. That was when a guy called Richard Henry began tracking and catching kiwi and kākāpō on the mainland and moving them to Resolution Island in Fiordland, because he could see the impact that stoats and ferrets were having on their populations.

Henry was one of the very first people in the world to use a dog for conservation purposes. He used to stick a muzzle and a bell on one of his dogs, and send it out to pick up the scent of the birds. Henry would follow the sound of the bell through the forest and eventually they would track down the birds. That's not so different to how I work with Ajax nowadays.

Henry's efforts to rescue the birds came to nothing eventually, as the island was within swimming distance for the mustelids. They eventually made their way across and wiped out his precious birds.

But his methods of tracking have gone on to have a massive impact on conservation work.

While Ajax is a bit of a trailblazer as a kea dog, some of this country's other parrots have also benefited from canines trained to find them. In fact, without conservation dogs, it's entirely possible that kākāpō would now be extinct. Much of their survival is down to a bloke called Gary Aburn and his dogs Jasper, Mandy and Boss. In the late 1970s and early 1980s, the four of them lived and worked on Stewart Island, where kākāpō were getting absolutely slammed by feral cats. Aburn spent a lot of his time trapping and poisoning the cats in order to give the kākāpō a chance to breed. They did, and in April 1980 Aburn and the dogs managed to track and make the first capture of a female kākāpō in about 70 years. This was significant because a lot of people believed there were no female kākāpō left. This bird was then transferred to Codfish Island, and it went on to play a major part in re-establishing the kākāpō population.

Aburn and the dogs went on to catch another 44 Stewart Island kākāpō over the next few years, with 14 of them being females— something he put down to the fact that the dogs had seen and smelled kākāpō in the bush and knew that he wanted them to find them. This proved to be a real turning point, not only for kākāpō but also for the use of dogs in conservation work. Nowadays, the department has around 80 dogs working for it in conservation roles—including, of course, Ajax.

Within the Conservation Dogs Programme, which has been running since 2002, there are two sub-programmes. There's the species-dog programme, for the dogs that are trained to find kiwi, whio, pāteke, kakī, penguins and, of course, kea. Dogs can be trained to find pretty much any ground-nesting bird. (You could probably train them to find birds in trees, too, but the ground-nesting ones are much easier to target.) Once we find the birds we're looking for, they are banded and monitored or, in the case of some rarer species, moved to other places where they'll be safe from predation. As well as birds, the dogs have been used to find skinks, geckos, frogs and even whitebait!

Ajax and Woody, a predator dog, on the job in Mount Cook National Park.

The dogs doing this sort of work tend to be indicator dogs, like pointers. There's a wide variety of dogs that are certified for conservation work and the bigger ones seem to be on the species side of things.

The other sub-programme is for dogs trained to sniff out predators or pest species. They're trained to find predators like cats, stoats, hedgehogs, mice, ferrets, weasels and rats. They can also be trained to find certain threat insects, like Argentine ants, or invasive weeds.

It's these dogs that get taken onto predator-free offshore islands if there have been reports of sightings of rats or other animals. They're especially useful in these sort of situations where predator numbers are low or their presence hasn't been confirmed, as they are able to track their prey really quickly.

These dogs are trained to track their target species. When they find them, they'll dig them out if necessary. Then the pest is killed using traps, shooting or poison.

The dogs have much the same role as the species dogs, but with a different target and a slightly different end result. Most of the predator dogs are little dogs, like fox terriers, Jack Russells and other small hunting dogs. They can get down into burrows and squeeze themselves into small spaces. They also have a different temperament to the dogs in the species–dog programme.

New Zealand leads the world in using dogs for conservation work—so much so that there's quite a bit of demand overseas for dogs that are trained here, and other governments are pretty interested in how our programme works.

Before any dog is allowed to undertake work on conservation projects, on public conservation land or in the presence of protected species, they have to go through a lot of training, just like I did with Ajax. Once I decided Ajax was ready to start work, he had to go through some rigorous testing. That process takes about 18 months.

The first test for the handler and the dog is to prove that the dog has mastered basic obedience skills. If you pass that one, you get another six months to train for the second test, which is held out in the field with the target species if possible.

If you fail the first test (called the interim test), you can get reassessed within three months, but you only get one chance to re-sit, and if you fail again you're off the course.

After six months, the dog and the handler then go through another series of tests before they become fully certified. These tests are to prove that the dog is obedient when its handler commands it to do something, that the handler knows what they're doing, that the dog won't go after other birds or fiddle with traps or baits, and that the dog will actually target the species that they're meant to be looking for.

If you pass, a full certificate is issued and the handler and dog are able to work on conservation projects together. Full certification lasts for only three years before it needs to be renewed.

If the final certification test is failed, then it's the same as the interim test—you have one more chance to be reassessed within three months. Fail that and you're off the programme.

This might seem pretty strict, but DOC has a world-class reputation for its dog programme so the standards are high. I've done a bit of work in Australia and they've been a little slow in taking up dogs for conservation work, although they're starting to use them a bit more as predator dogs. They've got some catching up to do on the endangered species front!

CHAPTER FIVE

AJAX TAKES THE TEST

Ajax was about two years old by the time he'd mastered everything that he needed to know to sit the first test on his way towards becoming a conservation dog. I knew he was up to the task, but I was still a bit nervous when I put in the application. We'd both been working so hard to get him ready for it.

The local dog assessor was based in Blenheim, so he called me up and said to meet him at Pollard Park, which is where everyone takes their dogs to chase Frisbees and run around. Any time Ajax and I had been to a place like that was for him to play. We'd hop out of the car and I'd say, 'Off you go!' Ajax would run off and muck around with the other dogs while I sat and watched him. In his mind, this was the place we went so he could just be a regular dog along with the rest of them.

I knew that Ajax was always much more focused and did things more quickly when he knew he was about to get fed, so I decided not to feed him the night before, to make him keen for a feed and willing to do what he was told the following morning. But the plan to get him on his best behaviour unravelled the following morning. I'd decided we'd get to the park early, then I'd give Ajax a look at his breakfast, so he knew that once he'd done his job for the morning he'd have a nice bit of dog roll waiting for him.

It was the perfect plan . . . except for the fact that when we got to the park, half an hour early as planned, the assessor was already there. Shit. With the assessor watching me, there was no way I could be seen bribing Ajax with his breakfast. Ajax got out of the truck

Ajax negotiates a stream in
Kahurangi National Park.

and gave me a filthy look because he was hungry. This was not going to go well.

On the upside, in Ajax's mind anyway, at least I'd brought him to the park for a play. The park is basically a paddock of grass surrounded by some exotic trees. Ajax had no idea that he was there to do work, because I'd never asked him to do that before in that environment. Having a stranger standing there watching didn't help things any either.

I stood there trying to command him to do all these things that he could do the day before without thinking, but Ajax was all over the place. Making things worse was the fact that I knew if he didn't complete just one of the tasks he had to perform then the test was over and we'd failed.

I managed to get him through the first couple of tasks: quietly walking on a lead while I changed directions a couple of times, then doing the same without a lead. After that, Ajax sat distractedly when I told him to. He even managed the whole 'stay' followed by 'come' process, even though he was a bit uncertain about it. Maybe—just maybe—this wasn't going to be a complete disaster.

Oh, but then came task number five: 'Dog will remain on a wait/ stay command while handler walks out of sight for 30 seconds before returning.'

All Ajax had to do was sit and stay while I went out of view for half a minute. He was meant to sit there and wait until I came back. I'd been gone for only a few seconds, and he was like, 'Oh! Where's he gone?', and came straight to where I was waiting. That was it. The assessor looked at me, shrugged and said, 'That's a fail.'

The only blessing was that we didn't have to continue the rest of the test, which included me fitting a muzzle on Ajax, and a section called 'Dog manners'. I didn't think that was going to go well.

I felt sad for Ajax because he was so confused. You would have thought he was a completely different dog compared to how he'd been even the day before. I was so frustrated. I would never have put him up for the test if I hadn't really believed that he could pass. All this hard work we'd both put in and he had failed. No, *we* had failed.

The dog assessor made it quite clear he believed that Ajax didn't have what it took. Thankfully, we had another chance to sit the test before Ajax would be kicked off the programme. Ajax, of course, wasn't too worried about this, as he was busy concentrating on his breakfast. We went home and I spent a bit of time trying to work out all the things that had gone wrong.

Ajax and I kept training for the three months that we'd been given before we could re-sit the test. It was quite weird having to keep going over and over all this stuff that he'd been doing perfectly all along. The one thing I did add to Ajax's training was getting him to do all of the tasks required of him in different environments, just in case we got thrown another curveball when it came to the location of the next test. But then I had a really good idea.

I decided to ask the assessor to come out to a place that was similar to where Ajax had learned to work and that he would associate with work. I decided on a spot out at St Arnaud, near the Nelson Lakes, where we'd done a lot of his training. It was more Ajax's and my turf than the dog park could ever be. Eventually, when I was confident that Ajax had all the tasks nailed, I got in touch with the assessor and thankfully he agreed to come out and meet us.

The day before we were due to do the test, I talked to a guy who had been through the whole testing process with his dog a few weeks beforehand. He told me that to pass the test, Ajax needed to be trained on the whistle. WHAT?! I hadn't read that anywhere in the manual. But the guy was adamant: 'I've just done my test and I didn't have any whistle commands and they said it wasn't good enough.'

We couldn't afford to fail the test again, so there was only one thing for it. I took Ajax down to the local park that evening and started training him on the whistle. It didn't take him long before he knew exactly which command went with which whistle noise. I was really impressed that he was able to pick up all the different whistle commands in one evening, and I slept a bit better that night.

The next morning, Ajax and I hopped in the truck and headed up to St Arnaud to meet the assessor. When we got there, Ajax jumped out of the truck and went straight over to the assessor. I was really

Ajax on White Horse Hill in Mount Cook National Park.

nervous, as it was our last chance to impress the guy. He looked at Ajax, who was giving him a friendly sniff, looked over at me, then said: 'This is a terrible sign. I don't think your dog is going to pass this test.'

'He just likes new people . . .' I tried to say, but the assessor wasn't having a bar of it. It was the first time that Ajax's friendly, calm nature had ever worked against him.

The next few minutes were incredibly nerve-wracking for me, but Ajax seemed completely unfazed by anything I threw at him during the test. While I felt a little bit like the assessor was out to fail my dog, and I couldn't do anything about it other than do my best, Ajax was quite happy to be out there doing what I wanted him to.

The assessor really put Ajax through his paces, and thankfully the little fella did everything absolutely perfectly. When I got the final report back from the test, it turned out that Ajax had got really high marks. He'd absolutely aced the whole test!

I was even a little bit disappointed that he didn't get put through a whistle test. When I told the assessor that I'd taught Ajax the whistle commands, he didn't seem interested in testing them out. I reckon the other guy had only got tested on them because he was working with a different assessor. The funny thing is that having spent that night training him on the whistle commands, we use them all the time now.

Having got that test under his belt (collar), we now had six months' more training to do before Ajax had to sit the final big test. If he passed that, he would be admitted to the Conservation Dogs Programme.

An adult male kea has a good scratch.

THREATS TO KEA

Think about the creatures that will adapt to eat pretty much anything. The list includes humans, rats, macaques, ravens, crows . . . and kea. The one thing all these creatures have in common is that they're all really smart. Animals that tend to eat only one thing—be it a plant, a type of seed or a type of meat—tend to be less smart, and they also tend to be lagging behind in terms of evolution. For kea, this adaptability around food has been the key to their survival, but it has also been a big part of their downfall.

Kea used to be a common sight in a lot of places where people interacted with the outdoors in the Southern Alps. Those interactions are happening less and less. That's partly because kea are being discouraged from those areas, and people are being discouraged from feeding them. It's also because we're changing the way we deal with our refuse. Dumps, where the birds might have scavenged, are being closed, which means the birds don't come into contact with humans there. They are becoming less and less visible because they're not being habituated to different food sources the way they used to be. That said, they're also becoming less visible because their numbers have been in decline. There are quite a few different reasons for this.

Introduced predators

The main predator impacting the kea population is the stoat. We know that kea are really productive—one breeding pair we know of has had four chicks in a single season. If kea were free from predators, they'd be able to increase their population really easily. In a stoat-plague year, the year after a beech-mast season, there's a pretty slim chance that any chicks will survive if there is no pest control. Through our research we've found that even in areas where there is widespread predator control, on average only 1.6 chicks per brood survive.

A good example of what could happen to kea can be seen in the case of the kākāpō. It used to be a hugely abundant bird, but it got wiped off the mainland largely because of stoats.

Kea are very similar in their nesting behaviours to kākāpō. They both nest on the ground, which makes them really vulnerable. We need to look to the lessons from the kākāpō when it comes to working to protect the kea. It was almost too late for the kākāpō, which are now found only on offshore islands. The kea have the benefit of breeding more regularly than the kākāpō, and that's the only thing that has kept them afloat compared to their more rare cousins.

Like the kākāpō, the kea tends to nest in a hole in the ground, which means a predator can get to the nest easily. The kea doesn't have the benefit of a nest in the top of a tree that a cat or a stoat might struggle to get to. There are one or two kea we know of that have been found in holes higher up in trees, but even those were within the range of a stoat.

Aside from the stoat, wild cats going into kea habitat will kill the birds. Possums will also kill kea and disturb their nests—they like to sleep in the same cavities that kea nest in—and rats have been seen hooking into kea eggs.

Direct human interference

The kea's intelligence and natural curiosity often sees them come into conflict with people who live in or utilise the South Island's alpine areas. In one of the worst cases that I've heard of, five dead kea were found piled up on a picnic table at Klondyke Corner, near the edge of Arthur's Pass National Park, in August 2011. It was made all that much worse when DOC workers realised that all five of them had been shot. A reward was offered for any information about who shot them, but no one was ever caught.

Nearer home for me, there are kea coming into places like Kaiteriteri and Murchison. People dislike them because they're rowdy and they wreck stuff. A lot of people in the northern part of the South Island are getting upset that kea are turning up in coastal areas. They say they've been there for ten or 20 years and there have never been any kea there before. They don't realise that the birds *used* to be there—it was part of their range but they've slowly been forced into smaller and smaller areas. Whenever we do get a great breeding year, the juveniles will explore further out because of the pressure on territory. People then say, 'Well, we don't want them here.' It's hard for me to understand that mentality.

There are people who do live very well with kea, and they're some of our best ambassadors. We had a great meeting at one of the pubs in Kaiteriteri to talk about some issues people had been having with a group of kea that were causing a bit of mayhem in a caravan park. The birds were landing on caravan roofs in the middle of the night and investigating their TV cables. People would turn on the lights then bang on the roof of the caravan and make lots of noise to try to scare the birds away. Of course, the kea thought this was a great lark. They absolutely loved the light and the noise, which made them even noisier.

We ended up with about 60 people at this meeting, and the room was pretty much divided half in half. One lot were saying that they thought it was so great to finally be seeing kea here again after so long. The other half were saying stuff like, 'The only good kea is a dead kea.' It was as upfront as that.

It turned out that the people who tolerated the kea and liked having them around were able to adapt and had been kea-proofing their properties without thinking about it too much. Some of them had even made play pits for the kea. They didn't put food out or anything—just a bunch of stuff that they knew the kea would love to explore and play with and that wouldn't hurt them. They allowed the birds that area, and they covered anything that they didn't want the kea to damage. The people who did that said that they loved to watch the birds playing.

We asked those people to talk to their neighbours and help them to kea-proof their properties. They were delighted to help, and the neighbours were glad of the advice. It's that kind of thing where communities are working together that will really help the birds. It also stops bad behaviour—people who might be a threat to kea know that their neighbours care about the birds and will know if something happens to them.

Despite all that, some people don't want to have to change; they want to be able to leave their rubbish out, rather than picking it up and putting it in a bin that the birds can't get into. They won't do anything that will either cost them money or time and effort. It would take only small changes for these people to be able to live harmoniously alongside birds that are becoming rarer all the time.

If people do have issues with kea around their properties, rather than take things into their own hands I'd really encourage them to contact either DOC or the Kea Conservation Trust so we can talk to them about things that they can do to minimise damage by the birds and to discourage them from coming into contact with humans.

A couple of times I've been called in to move kea because the locals have threatened to shoot them. I hate having to do it, and will do so only as an absolute last resort. The problem is that the birds don't cope that well with being moved. We caught six of them at Murchison and I took them about 100 kilometres away to release them. They had been living as a group, but when I released them they all went their different ways. Who knows where they ended up?

Word then got out that I'd moved the kea, and DOC started getting phone calls from people asking them to come and get weka off their properties. They even had calls from people wanting them to move little blue penguins because the birds had been making noise under their house! I've got weka at my place, and they pull plants out all the time. I just keep picking the plants up and putting them back in. It's all part and parcel of living in a rural area.

We're only too happy to help avoid situations where people decide to take things into their own hands. The birds have so much pressure on them. They still get shot—people shoot them all the time. Someone's just been convicted in Tākaka for shooting and killing a kea on his property with a .22 air rifle. He only admitted to killing one bird, but he said that there had been about eight causing damage at his property. He got 200 hours' community service.

These birds are absolutely protected and the maximum sentence for killing them is a $100,000 fine and two years in prison. The legislation that covers the killing of native birds is pretty strong, but

A pair of adult kea in Kahurangi National Park. My friend and colleague Liam Bolitho can be seen in the background.

there have been only two convictions for people killing kea in recent years. Given how often we hear of them being deliberately harmed that doesn't seem enough.

Kea hang out in flocks, so if someone does shoot and kill seven or eight of them, that's the entire flock gone from that place. They're usually really social birds except for when they're breeding, when they become very territorial. If they breed on a particular hill, that's their hill and they'll protect it. If you shoot them in their breeding territory or they die there, it's going to take a long time before another kea will find that nesting spot and establish themselves there.

Lead poisoning

Lead poisoning is a real problem for kea in the wild. Lead was used as a building material a lot last century, and its presence is still common in old buildings in kea habitats such as sheds, cribs or baches and huts. Lead-head nails and lead flashing around chimneys and along rooflines are the biggest problems. Thankfully lead's not used in building anymore, but there's still a lot of it out there in the ski fields and old huts in places like Arthur's Pass.

We do our best to get people who live in kea habitat to seal lead or replace it on their houses. Public buildings are a bit more tricky as there are a whole lot of health and safety aspects that have to be taken into account, which makes it way more expensive, but it's happening gradually.

Kea can also get lead from car-tyre weights, which clip onto the rims. The birds have worked out how to pop them off easily.

Lead is soft and malleable, and it tastes sweet to the birds. They only need a tiny little flake of lead and they can be poisoned. It stuffs them up really badly. It disrupts their reproductive cycle, causes cognitive problems, and in severe cases can result in death. It also messes with their digestive systems and replaces calcium in their bones and eggs, so these are much weaker. When you've got lead replacing calcium, the eggs aren't strong enough to survive through to hatching.

Other human activity

Kea that live in close proximity to humans have been shown to be more at risk of death than kea in the wild. This is because they are more likely to eat rubbish that is toxic to them.

Hanging around in carparks also brings added risk for the birds. There have been cases of them getting stuck in rubbish bins. But more lethal is the fact that they become habituated to cars being around, and this leads to them being killed by vehicle strike.

One of the real hotspots for this kind of thing is around Arthur's Pass. Every year at least a couple of birds get killed in the area. In 2016, two were found on the same weekend. One, called Xaphod, was thought to have been hit by a car in the Temple Basin ski field carpark, while another young female kea was found dead outside the Bealey Hotel.

Around the same time the following year, another two birds were found dead on the same weekend. They had both been hit by vehicles near Death's Corner, by the Ōtira Viaduct lookout. There were about 20 birds in the area at the time. The birds are drawn to the carpark there because people feed them, which puts them at greater risk of getting run over. There are big signs there now explaining that kea should be left alone, so hopefully that will make a difference. (Even though the signs look as if the birds have already had a good chew on them!)

Part of the reason the kea are at risk on the roads is that they tend to hop over the road instead of fly. On the open road, this makes them a sitting target for fast-moving cars.

The only real solution to this is for drivers to slow down when they're driving through areas where kea are known to congregate. One thing that has helped to prevent road deaths are warning signs that have been put up through the Arthur's Pass area to let motorists know that kea are around, and to ask them to slow down.

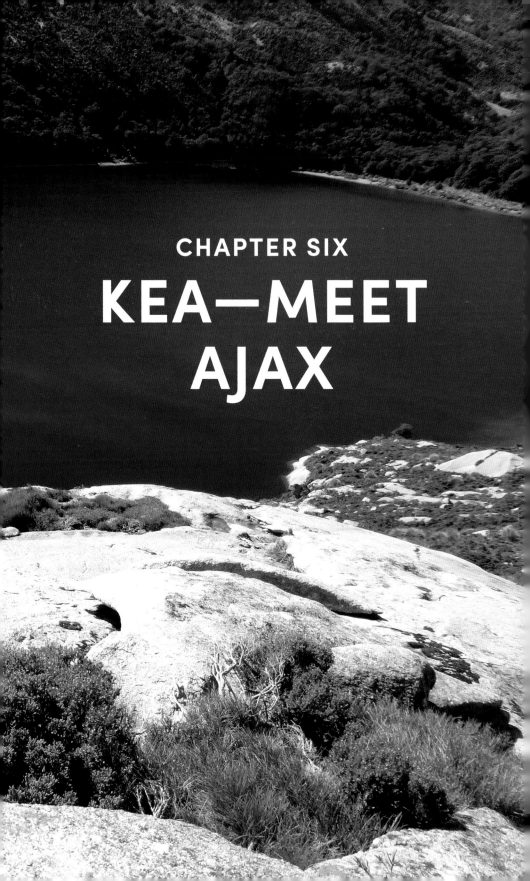

CHAPTER SIX

KEA—MEET AJAX

Ajax and I got an extension on the amount of time before we sat the second test because we had ended up taking the first test near the end of the kea season. Ajax would have had barely any time out in the field looking for nests if we'd stuck to the original timetable.

The reality is that we don't come across that many kea nests in our day-to-day work, and they're usually in quite rough terrain, so to train Ajax properly to seek them out, he needed plenty of time in the field to get him really homed in. I was pleased that we got the training time extended another few months, as it gave Ajax more time to get attuned to finding kea nests.

Before I could worry about the second test, though, it was time to introduce Ajax to kea for real. Up until then, we'd done quite a bit of work at home to get him interested in kea, using feathers and—slightly grossly—kea poo. Getting him keen on the kea scent was really important. Following footprints is one thing, but the best way to get him to indicate a kea nest is the acrid scent that emanates from the copious amount of kea poo scattered outside the entrance. They make quite a lot of mess just outside the nest, so fresh dung is a good indicator of an active nest. Because kea poo was what Ajax was ultimately out to find, I would often present him with clothes that I had worn in and around kea nests, as they carried that unique smell.

Quite often I'd come back from being in the hills and have kea poo all over my shirt. When I got home, I'd give him the shirt, tell him, 'This is a kea', then give him plenty of positive reinforcement in the form of praise and food.

Kea poo was a great thing to train him on. Ajax only needs to get a whiff of it now and he'll know exactly where a kea has been walking around. Now when I don't take him out to the hills and I come home smelling of kea, he gets a bit dark because he knows I've been out without him!

Because he'd passed his first test, Ajax was finally allowed to come into the national parks with me. But we didn't have to go very far to introduce him to the birds. That's because by this time we were living down at Arthur's Pass, where kea roam the streets with reckless abandon! Their scent is scattered all over the footpaths and they can be spotted regularly congregating in small gangs in the village carparks.

The fact that kea are so prolific near the town caused me to panic a bit when I got home one night to find Ajax had gone missing. I'd gone out to get some food and left him tied to a post outside the house. In the time that I'd been gone he'd managed to chew through where the rope was tied up and buggered off. I was a little bit worried that he might have taken himself off kea hunting.

I took off out to the road to see if I could find him. Thankfully, I didn't have to go far—I got about 20 metres down the road before I could hear him whining. I followed the noise and found Ajax over at a neighbour's place. He'd gone off with the rope dragging behind him and managed to get it wedged in some branches. The dog who was smart enough to escape being tied up at my place managed to tie himself up at the neighbour's. But he wasn't smart enough to work out how to do his escape act twice in a night!

While we were living at Arthur's Pass, all it took for Ajax to show interest in the birds' trails was some words of encouragement when he put his nose to the ground where kea had been. Up until this point, he'd only ever picked the smell of kea on things that I'd brought home—this was his first time sniffing out the actual birds.

I had one other kea-training plan up my sleeve. I got six plastic containers with lids on them and drilled small holes in the lids. In one of them I would put some kea nesting material, but I'd leave the rest empty. With Ajax out of view, I'd go and spread the containers all around the yard. Then I'd go and get Ajax and tell him to find the kea. He'd always go straight to the container with the nesting material in it.

This was a great way to train him to go looking for kea material, and it was also a great way for me to learn how Ajax would indicate to me that he'd found it. We were both learning about one another and how we each worked, which was pretty cool.

Finding kea paths along the roadside was a common pastime for me and Ajax during our evenings in Arthur's Pass village. But while we had easy access to plenty of kea, I still had a few things I had to teach Ajax.

One really important thing he had to learn was to leave things alone when I told him to. I first started doing it with his ball—I'd chuck it in front of him and tell him to leave it. He'd just sit there staring at it. Then I moved on to stopping him mid-stride when he was chasing the ball. No problem there. Once I knew he had the hang of the commands, I started using them with his food.

I'd put his dog roll right in front of him and tell him to leave it. As with the ball, he'd sit there staring at it, and every now and then he'd look at me to make sure I was still watching him. Eventually, I'd tell him to eat it. That progressed to letting him pick the food up in his mouth, then I'd tell him to leave it. He'd drop it and sit down. Then I'd let him have a bite, then command him to leave it. It was incredible to see how much self-control he had.

Gradually, I extended the amount of time that I'd get him to leave the food alone. I'd tell him to leave it, then I'd go inside for half an hour, and when I came back out he'd still be sitting there looking at the dog roll. There were a couple of times when I forgot that I'd left him there and got really engrossed in other work while I was inside. When I remembered about an hour and a half later, I'd go flying out to make sure he got his dinner and he'd still be sitting there with the dog roll untouched. I was so impressed with him and felt really proud that he'd done what I'd asked of him despite being quite hungry. I knew then that I would have no trouble when I finally introduced him to kea, because he'd just do what I asked him to do.

Ajax and I would often go up to the Death's Corner carpark overlooking the Ōtira Viaduct because heaps of kea would hang out there. The birds liked that spot because there were always cars and people for them to snaffle food from. The kea there were used to people, so they were particularly bold. Their natural curiosity came in handy in helping Ajax learn that the birds were something I was particularly interested in.

One technique I used up there—to show Ajax that kea were something that he should be interested in but also something that he shouldn't chase—was to put a small stone, a bit of feather or a little stick in between Ajax's toes. I then gave him two commands—'stay' and 'leave it'.

The first time I tried it, Ajax lay there looking at the new decoration on his feet and waited to see what would happen. Before long, a young kea, displaying a complete absence of fear as well as an ambitious inquisitiveness, ran straight up to him and plucked out the object from between his toes. Ajax didn't so much as flinch.

We did this lots of times, but no matter what happened Ajax would just sit there as the kea ran around him. Once they realised he wasn't going to do anything, they started to prod him with their beaks. The kea would cruise up and pull the bits of feather and stuff out from between his toes and he did nothing. He sat there with his feet out and let the kea muck around with them. He was muzzled, so even if they had bothered him too much he wouldn't have been able to open his mouth on them. But he really didn't care. That was so satisfying for me. It showed me that Ajax was well trained and ready to be out there in the forest.

One day, I left Ajax sitting in the truck with the window open while I went to do a couple of chores. I came back to find several kea on the roof of the truck, poking their faces into the cab where Ajax was sitting. He was just looking out at them and not reacting at all—even when one of the birds bit him on the septum of his nose. He recoiled slightly, a bit shocked at having been nipped, but he still didn't make a fuss. He was so chilled out around the birds.

His chilled-out nature has meant that he's really good at working

Ajax and an inquisitive kea at Death's Corner.

with birds. He doesn't get all excited when he's around them—he just cruises. The birds land on him all the time and it doesn't faze him at all. I've got a photo of him with a tiny robin sitting on his foot and he's quite happy.

Then there's the weka that love to peck at his toe pads when he's lying down having a snooze in the sun. I've seen weka in different places around the country all do exactly the same thing—they love the soft skin on the bottom of his feet. And Ajax? He'll just look at them, vaguely annoyed, but he doesn't bother getting up or doing anything to stop them. He can get feisty when he needs to, and sometimes he gets really pissed off, but that doesn't happen very often and not unless he's really being wound up.

It didn't take long before I knew that Ajax was well tuned to the birds and that he wasn't bothered by them. The other thing I had to make sure he could do was find the nests out in the bush.

A lot of kea nests are big enough that I can climb into them, so when he'd indicate an active nest, I'd climb in to check out who was home. If there wasn't anything in there, I'd call Ajax in to have a look around. He'd come in behind me and really take in what was inside the nest. I think it gave him some understanding of what it was I was looking for. Once he knew it was something that interested me then he was onto it straight away, and he'd sniff out nests because he knew he'd get rewarded with some big pats and lots of attention. Even though he's been into the nests with me, he still worries a little bit if I go into them without him. He has a wee whine when I'm in there to let me know he's outside waiting for me.

The funny thing about Ajax's job is that even though he is all about tracking kea, he very seldom has any interaction with the birds themselves. He never goes into a nest unless I've gone in first to make sure it's empty. If the nest is empty but he knows there are birds nearby, even then he doesn't often go near them. He'll head in their general direction, then make sure he has my full attention while he shows me where they are.

Ajax with a robin resting on his foot in Kahurangi National Park.

One other thing he's really good at finding are whio or blue ducks. I like taking photos, so whenever I hear the ducks I'll wander down to photograph them. Ajax has worked out that they are something I'm interested in, so quite often when we're walking along next to a river, he'll head off down to the water, indicating that he's found something.

His mellow personality means that he's really easy to be around, which makes working with him enjoyable. The puppy my flatmate brought home, his sister, had a much louder personality and, if I'm honest, I reckon being around her all the time would have driven me nuts.

The only time Ajax really even barks is when cars arrive at home. He'll be out on the driveway making a heap of noise, then when people get out of the car he's right there having a good look at them. He does scare the odd person who's not expecting his special form of greeting, but as soon as they're out of the car he'll be lining them up for a pat. I do have a command to make him bark, but it's not 'speak!', it's 'walkies!' He always barks when I say that because he gets a bit excited about going out.

Eventually, the nine months of training was up and it was time for Ajax to take the second test. I was pretty worried about what would happen to him if he didn't pass the test. Not only would I not have him there helping me to find nesting sites, I'd also have to worry about what he was getting up to when I wasn't home. I hated the thought of such an active dog not being allowed to come out and work with me in the forest every day.

The final test is really designed to show an assessor all the things we'd had to do in the first test, as well as how the dog works out in the field—how they indicate, how they behave when they find the target species, and how they work with their handler. To do this, we had to take an assessor into the bush with us and let Ajax do his job.

I managed to get away with not taking the assessor into the bush, as it's such a mission to get to active nests. If we'd taken him away into the Kahurangi and got to a nesting site only to find that there was nothing there because the nest had been predated, that wouldn't have been ideal. Instead, I took him to a nesting site that I knew of where there were no kea active at the time, so he could still see how Ajax reacted around kea indications.

When we got there, I talked about what I expected Ajax to do, and then showed him the dog in action. Ajax was happy to be working and did everything exactly as I wanted him to. He passed the test easily. Ajax was now a fully fledged Conservation Dog, and I couldn't wait to get out there with him and get to work.

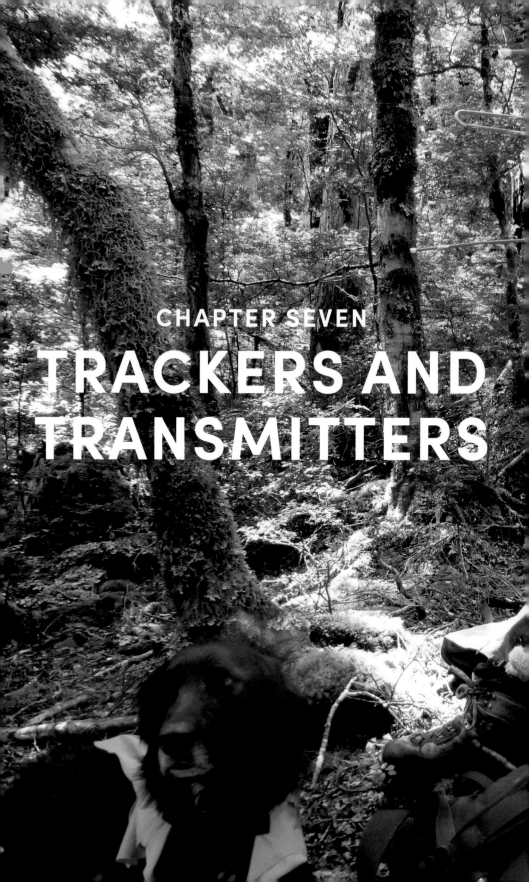

CHAPTER SEVEN

TRACKERS AND TRANSMITTERS

Our friend and volunteer Lindsay Skyner helps me attach a transmitter to a kea in Kahurangi National Park, with Ajax looking on. PHOTO BY PETE GREBOWSKI

All the time that Ajax and I had been doing his training, I was still doing my day job for the Kea Conservation Trust. I'd have to leave Ajax at home and go off out into the field. A big part of the work that I was doing—and that he was now going to join me doing—was monitoring kea nests.

To monitor a nest, first we need to know where it is. To find them, we use radio-frequency transmitters attached to the birds. We catch the birds in the summer when we're doing population surveys and fit them with transmitters, which attach to the kea like a little backpack. When the breeding season comes around, the transmitters are able to give us some indication of where to find the bird. We are mostly working adult females, as they're the ones sitting on the nests. Sometimes this can take me and Ajax on wild goose (kea) chases to very remote parts of various national parks.

The tracking can be done by aeroplane, but in Nelson Lakes we can start from the road to get a good idea of where the birds are, then Ajax and I will head in on foot to find them. As we get closer, I'll use a radio receiver to track down the birds from a high point, with a clear line of sight, and then we move in by following the signal as it intensifies.

Once the technology has helped us to narrow down the location of the nests, that's when Ajax gets to work. He can smell a kea from quite a long way away, and he'll drop his nose to the ground and go in search of the nest, eventually leading me right to its doorway.

While they're not quite as strong as Ajax's finely honed nose, the transmitters are a pretty cool piece of kit. They work a bit like a Fitbit or an app on your phone. Inside it there's an accelerometer, so we know when the birds are moving and not sitting on the nest. If the bird has been stationary for 12 hours, the signal of the transmitter will change to a double pulse. When we hear that, there are two options: either the bird is dead or the transmitter has fallen off. If the transmitter pulse-rate changes from 20 pulses per minute to 40 pulses per minute it means the bird is nesting. Once we see that, Ajax and I can go in and set up cameras around the nest so we can monitor it.

The technology was developed by a couple of guys called John Wilks and Alastair Bramley, who started a company called Wildtech. It's quite a cool story. John and Alastair first ran into each other at a meeting at their local Playcentre in Havelock North. They got talking and discovered they had a mutual interest in both conservation and technology. In that classic Kiwi way, the two of them ended up in a garage experimenting with a few ideas about how to improve kiwi-tracking technology based on an understanding of the birds' behaviour. For expert advice, they got kiwi guru Dr John McLennan on board.

Up until this point, kiwi and other birds had been fitted with transmitters that could only be monitored at close range, so workers had to go into the bush every couple of weeks and actually sit there waiting for the birds to do stuff. What happened in between times was anybody's (educated) guess.

A bit of beer drinking and a lot of thinking then led to the development of what John and Alastair called the 'Egg Timer' transmitter in 2005. These original transmitters were so accurate that workers could tell exactly how long a bird had been incubating an egg for, so that if necessary DOC staff could go in and pick the eggs up for safe hatching in incubators. One of the amazing things about the technology is that it cost about $40,000 to develop, but ended up saving about $160,000 for every 100 kiwi monitored by it.

The transmitter technology was first used for kiwi, but has since been adjusted so that it can be used on kākā, kākāpō, takahē, tāiko, weka and, of course, kea. They've even developed one for use on possums. As well as measuring activity, like they do for the kea, they can also measure daylight levels—this is particularly useful when tracking kākā, because they nest deep inside hollow trees where there is no light—and mating interactions (it can pick up the particular sequence of movements that the bird makes only when it's mating and not at any other time during its day).

The transmitter sits on the bird's back, attached to a harness. Where the harness joins together on the bird's breast, there's a deliberate weak link, made of cotton and covered with plastic. It's designed so that the cotton will wear out over time, and eventually the whole harness falls apart and comes off the bird. This means that if you can't catch that bird again, it won't be burdened with the transmitter forever—at some point, it will just drop off.

The birds can and do chew them off, but if that's going to happen it'll usually be within a few days of us putting them on. We know that when we get mortality outputs suggesting the bird isn't moving really soon after a harness has been attached, it's usually because the bird has managed to get it off. Sometimes as soon as I put the harness on the bird is straight into it, trying to take it off. If that happens I do my best to distract them, by making some noise or wriggling something colourful or noisy at them. That's usually enough to make them forget about their new bit of kit.

The transmitters don't seem to affect the birds at all. The birds can fly without difficulty and the transmitters don't stop the birds from breeding. Obviously they are a slight burden for an individual bird, but the amount of information we can get out of the transmitters makes it worthwhile.

As well as the transmitter technology, John and Alastair also developed the aerial monitoring system we use, which is called Sky Ranger. Using planes to track the transmitter signals achieves in two hours what would, in the past, have taken nearly two whole days on the ground.

A fixed-wing aircraft can cover quite a large area in a short amount of time, and it's way cheaper than using helicopters. The planes fly a grid pattern, using a computer program to track the frequencies on the transmitters and where the signals are coming from. This is translated into map data, showing us the location of the transmitters, which is incredibly accurate. From the data, we can work out whether the birds are nesting, then Ajax and I head in on foot to find the nests.

When we're in the field we use portable trackers that kind of look like old TV aerials, and we depend on a line of sight to be able to pick up the radio signal being transmitted. When you're close to the birds but in the next valley over, or on the other side of a hill, you won't get any signal. As soon as you get to the ridge, or in a clear line to the transmitter, you'll pick them up easily.

Once when I was out tracking birds up near the top of the Pearse Ridge, out the back of Tapawera, which is part of Kahurangi National Park, I picked up a signal from Nelson Lakes, more than 50 kilometres away. I thought, *surely not*, but then the machine started giving an output. For a minute I thought it must have been a clashing frequency from some other species, like a kiwi, that happened to be in the area, but I checked on the GPS and it was 65 kilometres in a straight line across to where the signal was coming from. It just goes to show how clear a VHF radio signal can be, and how useful the trackers are. Not even Ajax could sniff out a kea at that distance!

As with any skill, it took Ajax a while to really get the hang of what his job was when it came to searching for kea in the wild. The only way for him to learn was for him to come out with me and do it. That meant that I took him on as many trips as I could, as he gradually added to his repertoire of skills and his understanding of what I wanted him to do.

Not all of these trips were super straightforward, and it took him a while to get the hang of what he was meant to be doing. I had one particularly nerve-wracking trip early on, when we were catching kea up near the Baton Saddle in Kahurangi National Park. After a night camping, Ajax and I were walking back down the hill to the trail head. As we made our way down, Ajax got on the scent of

A sub-adult male kea pops up and surprises Ajax in Kahurangi National Park.

something and took off. I wasn't too worried about him because he had his muzzle on and I knew he'd come back to me if he found a bird—at least I thought he would.

I waited for about ten minutes and started to wonder where he was. Then I started to worry a little bit, so began calling him. I lost count of how many times I yelled 'AJAX!' After about an hour and a half, I'd managed to lose both my dog and my voice. It slowly dawned on me that there was nothing more I could do. It was getting late and I had no idea where he was.

There was nothing for it but to head back towards the truck. It was a tough decision to make, and all I could do was trust that he'd be able to track my scent back down to the carpark. I really hoped that, if he got on the scent, he'd follow it the right way and wouldn't head back up into the hills. Being muzzled meant he wouldn't be able to eat anything, so his survival really depended on him making the right choice of which scent to follow.

Then, just as I chucked my pack on my back, who should turn up but Ajax. He was super puffed but was looking very pleased with himself. I was so relieved, but also annoyed at him for running away. I couldn't tell him off, though, because he would have thought he was being growled at for coming back. Never have I called him a 'good boy' in a less convincing way!

On another of Ajax's earliest trips out into Kahurangi National Park, we were off in search of a bird whose transmitter had gone into mortality mode. We were prepared to become forensic investigators in order to hunt down its dead body, but when we're on these missions we're always hoping that the bird is fine and that we will recover a dropped transmitter instead.

I knew that the terrain would be quite challenging for Ajax—it was a bit of a step up in terms of difficulty from what we'd covered before. It would be a good chance for him to experience some pretty rugged conditions and also to help me scout out the missing bird if it was still alive.

We headed towards the signal, which took us to the Nuggety Creek track, in the valley over from the Wangapeka River. We walked for about two hours along the track, following the river up the valley, with the shadow of Mount Owen looming over us. On this day we also had a volunteer and a trainee worker with us.

For all of us, this was a form of training in how to locate kea: the humans with telemetry gear (the TV aerial things) and the dog with his nose. We arrived at the top of the track, about 1200 metres above sea level, and got a very clear signal. It seemed to be just a few hundred metres away. It was looking like the mission was going to be quite a quick one—I reckoned that we'd have the signal chased down within half an hour or so and then, with Ajax on the job, the kea found minutes later. Alas, it was not to be.

We walked to the edge of a limestone cliff only to find that the signal was further down, possibly on the valley floor. That was all well and good, except for the fact that there was absolutely no way down into the valley from where we were standing. We returned to the track that we'd come in on, and this eventually wound us down into the next valley over.

On the way down, we stopped at a known kea-nest cavity that we knew the bird we were looking for used to frequent, so we were hoping that it might be there waiting for us. Ajax headed off on the scent, but didn't give his usual signal to indicate that he had found live birds. He was bang on: the nest contained only a few feathers and sticks arranged in the shape of a small bowl, ideal for housing eggs for incubation—but there were none there.

Disappointed not to have found any birds at home, I retrieved the motion-sensitive camera from outside the entrance to the nest cavity. It had been installed to monitor all the comings and goings at this particular nest throughout the breeding season. From the footage that these cameras record, we can tell how successful a kea nest has been (how many chicks have survived to fledge), and compare it to known predator levels in that particular area. This helps us to determine the likely survival of fledglings from that nest.

Having eaten our lunch, we continued down to the valley floor and across into the next valley, where the transmitter signal seemed to be coming from. Once there we followed the stream, as I constantly

Ajax looks out from Woolshed Hill
in Arthur's Pass National Park.

checked the signal from the transmitter. It kept indicating that it was further downstream, so we carried on in that direction.

Occasionally the stream completely disappeared. Being in limestone country, this means caves and underground waterways, so we had to be careful to avoid any hidden sumps along the way. Eventually the stream became a constant flow, but it got way harder to follow as the boulders got bigger and the climbing got steeper. An old track marker gave us hope that there was a way out in the direction we were heading.

While the three humans enjoyed the challenge of navigating the boulders as we made our way downstream, it was more difficult for Ajax, because he was much lower to the ground and big rocks were not so easy to bound over and slide down. Credit where it's due, though—Ajax kept up with us and didn't seem too bothered by the challenging terrain.

Eventually the signal on the radio receiver intensified to indicate that we were very close to the transmitter. We stopped to check the direction that the signal was coming from. It was pointing straight back up to the cliffs we had been standing on top of an hour or so earlier! Damn.

We had a bit of a talk about it, and came to the conclusion that the transmitter must have been sitting somewhere in the middle of the cliff. There was no way that any of us—dog or human—was going up there to try to get it. The only thing left to do now was to find our way back out of the valley and head home. Easier said than done.

Not wanting to backtrack the way we had come, we decided to keep on heading down the stream. More redundant track markers increased our confidence and our drive to continue on.

Ajax didn't get a say on our plan of action, but his actions suggested he would prefer to go against the majority. Slippery boulders are unfriendly surfaces for anyone to walk on, but when you have claws they are a lot more difficult to negotiate. The poor dog didn't know what he was in for at the start of the day, and now found himself being constantly manhandled, passed from one person to another down the narrow, boulder-filled canyon.

Huge, vertical cliffs hung over pristine, sapphire-blue cascades of flowing water as we made our way downstream. It was absolutely stunning to explore, and was topped off at one point by the whistle and territorial display of a male whio underneath one of the numerous waterfalls in the area. It provided quite a show for all of us.

The space between the cliffs had been getting narrower for a while, but we kept going. Further down what was obviously once a track but no longer existed on maps—for understandable reasons—we got to a point where there were cliffs on both sides of us and a great big boulder right in the middle that we couldn't go over or around. I thought we'd have to go all the way back up the canyon to get out, but one of the other guys saw that there was a tiny old wire caver's ladder bolted into the rock, draping its way down the moss-laden surface into a crystal-clear pool below. It was too high to jump from the top of the boulder into the stream beyond, so in order to get down we needed the ladder.

My mate yanked on the ladder and said, 'She'll be right.'

I wasn't so sure. 'You test it out first then!'

Fortunately, we humans got down there no worries. But when there is a creature without hands involved, things are a lot more difficult. I had to work out how we were going to get Ajax down.

Luckily there was also an old, slightly mouldy rope tied next to the wire ladder. I made the rope into a harness around Ajax's waist, then tied it back through his collar with a few safety knots and doubled the rope back in on itself to make it more secure.

One of the other guys was at the bottom and I was at the top of the ladder. I told him I'd dangle Ajax down to him. Ajax wasn't that keen on the plan—he got to the edge of the boulder and then dug his toes in. He wasn't having a bar of it. He managed to wedge himself under the rope and made it quite clear he didn't want to go anywhere. There was a brief period where I was astounded at how well a dog without fingers to grip with could hold on to a piece of scrub so well and not be budged. I kept holding onto the rope, trying to push him over with my foot.

Eventually, I managed to nudge him off the edge and the other

Ajax on one of his other adventures: a canyoning trip with our friends Dale Clark and Anna Jakobsmeier in Kahurangi National Park.

guy grabbed him at the bottom, slowly lifting him down before untying him. After all Ajax's protesting, it ended up being a very straightforward manoeuvre!

Fortunately for all of us—but especially Ajax—this was the hardest obstacle that we had to overcome that day. But there were still another couple of surprises in store before we made it home.

We carried on down the gorge into a big canyon where the river started flowing again. At one point, there was a bit of a slide down some rocks. Ajax looked at me as if to say, 'What now?', so I said, 'Wait there! Wait there!' But he decided he knew better and wasn't going to listen to me. He slid off down these rocks, trying his best to hold on, but when he got to the end he just popped off and went straight into the river. Once I knew he was OK, I laughed and said, 'Well, I did tell you to stay there!'

There was one spot not much further on where the stream hit the track again. This meant we had to wade through several deep pools in the river. That was fine for those of us on two legs, even though the water was up to our necks in some places. At one point I decided to let go, and was suspended with my feet floating above the sandy, shingly bottom of the river. It was strangely peaceful.

For Ajax, though, the water obstacles meant he had to swim. This took a bit of persuading from me and the rest of the team, but eventually he realised he had no choice and hopped in the water. He swam along until he reached a log in the river, then he climbed up onto the log and stood on it, looking at me as if to say, 'That's it. I've had enough.'

It was hard for me seeing his bedraggled little body shivering away, but I knew the best thing for him (and the rest of us) was to get back to the truck as quickly as we could. I grabbed him off the log and chucked him back in the river, so he could swim to the shore and clamber back up onto the riverbank. When we got back to the carpark and hopped in the truck, Ajax wasn't the only one who was really happy!

For Ajax, trips like this where he had to do new stuff helped him to learn new skills, and also reinforced to him that he could trust me.

Even though he was a bit uncomfortable at times, he soon realised that I would always look out for him. He learned that when we were going up cliffs where you really need hands to hold on, where it's steep or where there's a bit of rock that you have to clamber around, I would always help him. I quickly learned how to position myself so that he knew I was there to get him up or down boulders, banks or other steep drops. He also learned to wait until I was ready to help him.

For example, there'd be places where he'd watch me hop up onto, say, a ledge above him. He knew that he couldn't leap that far, but he soon worked out that he could jump up high enough so that I could grab his collar. Once he'd got that sussed out, our trips out into the high country were much easier. He'd wait until I was ready for him and then hop up so I could grab him and pull him up. He's got really good at trusting that I'll get him to any place he can't climb to himself.

On the way down, however, he finds it a lot harder to trust that I've got him. Sometimes he'll whine a little bit on the downhills, over steep slopes or rocky drops. There have been a few times when I've climbed down off a ledge and will get myself into position to help him down. He'll be standing above me, away from the edge, and I have to try to get him to come towards it. He just doesn't want to do it because he's a bit scared. Sometimes he'll take off and try to find his own way down, because he thinks he knows better than me. I usually have to climb back up and manhandle him down. Going up he's perfect, but coming down he doesn't feel quite so secure. It's the same for humans, I guess—most of us feel much safer climbing up than heading down hills.

After our epic trip into the Kahurangi, a couple of quite cool things happened. One was that we got a special harness made for Ajax, so that if he needs to be lowered down like that again, he can be safe and a lot more comfortable. He's come back up to that same canyon with me since, and now we both know what to expect, it's much easier to navigate. He's even quite happy to be lowered down the ladder as long as he's got his new harness on.

Back at the office, I reviewed the footage from the camera that had been filming the activity outside the nest that we'd visited. From those recordings, I was able to determine that the transmitter we were after that day had indeed fallen off the kea, so it probably was sitting in a rock crevice somewhere up that massive cliff. The reason I knew this was that the footage contained brilliant, full-colour pictures of the adult male kea that transmitter belonged to—and they were taken a whole month after the date that the transmitter had gone into mortality mode. He was alive and well after all, so that made the whole adventure worthwhile, I reckon!

Oh, and since then Ajax has really learned to love swimming. He proved that when we were working up in the Douglas Range, which links the Aorere Valley—near where the Heaphy Track starts—to the Cobb Valley out the back of Tākaka. There's a track up to Boulder Lake, where there's an eight-bunk DOC hut. It's quite a cool walk to get up there: the first 5 kilometres or so are easy, then you climb up through beech and mānuka onto a pretty exposed saddle called Brown Cow. From there you have to head across the top of a big scree slope before heading down through the tussocks to the lake itself. To get to the hut, you have to walk right along the eastern side of the lake.

It's a good six- or seven-hour hike to get up there, with a few deviations off the track to check kea nesting sites. This one day we were up there, it was absolutely stinking hot. As we started walking along beside the lake, I heard a bit of a splash. Ajax had spotted the hut, worked out that was where we were heading and decided to swim there. He happily paddled alongside me as I carried on walking.

What he hadn't quite factored in was that he can't swim quite as fast as I can walk, and eventually he ended up lagging a fair way behind me. I waited for him to catch up a couple of times, but realised that we'd take all afternoon at the pace he was swimming. I called back to him, 'Get on the track!', and he climbed out of the water, gave himself a good shake and—slightly grudgingly—walked the rest of the way to the hut.

Me and Ajax at Boulder Lake
in Kahurangi National Park.
PHOTO BY MITCH BARTLETT

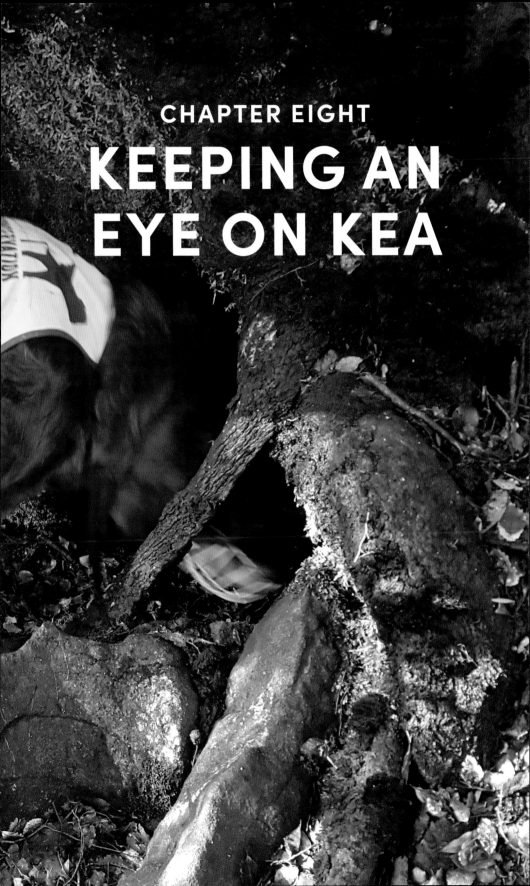

CHAPTER EIGHT

KEEPING AN EYE ON KEA

An adult male kea perches on some mountain beech.

Most of the work Ajax and I do is for the Kea Conservation Trust. We're part of a research team that monitors kea nests throughout the South Island, but we've got certain areas that we're focused on. To start with, the monitoring was used to make sure we were doing our population surveys at the right time: when the birds that have just fledged are learning to fly around the mountain tops, usually in January. Later we realised that the monitoring also gave us a lot of information on predation, how many nests had been successful in the area, and the development of nests and chicks through the year.

Most of the work we do is in the Kahurangi and Nelson Lakes national parks, but we sometimes work in the Hawdon Valley, near Arthur's Pass, down on the West Coast, around Mount Cook, and a bit in Fiordland. We've also started some monitoring down in the Mātukituki Valley near Wānaka. Pretty much wherever kea live, we'll be out there looking for them.

An average day for Ajax and me starts either at home or in a tent somewhere. If we're heading into the field from home, I always start early to make the most of the day. Quite often I'll have the alarm set for around 5 a.m. On mornings when I'm not heading into the hills, Ajax will get up when I get up. But when I have to get up early, he'll wake up, open his eyes, look up at me, then just put his head back down. If he could talk, he'd be saying, 'Yeah . . . nah.' Then he'll do his best to ignore me and go back to sleep. I know he really wants to come out with me but he also loves his sleep. (In fact, he loves his sleep so much that if he ever wakes me up in the night, I know that I have to get up and let him outside as fast as possible . . . or the results are likely to be very messy indeed. There have been a couple of times when I didn't get up quite quickly enough. Once he bolted out into the living room as soon as I opened the bedroom door, then vomited on the carpet.)

Eventually, Ajax will wander out to the kitchen after I've been mucking around for a while, making coffee and sorting out breakfast. I'll give him a feed of biscuits to get him ready for the day, and while he's eating I'll pack all the gear we need into the truck. Once that's done, Ajax will jump in the back of the truck and we're off.

It's often still dark as we head off from home, so Ajax makes the most of the drive to catch up on some more sleep. The night before we go, I'll have sussed out what ground I want to cover so I'll have a pretty good plan in my mind for the day. We're pretty lucky because we can access quite a few parts of the Kahurangi and Nelson Lakes national parks as well as quite a few other forest parks and bits of conservation land within about an hour's drive from my home base near Nelson.

As soon as we stop, Ajax'll be out of the truck and amping to go. The only part he's not a massive fan of is having his muzzle put on. He usually has a bit of a grizzle about this, but it's a vital piece of kit for any dog working in conservation areas. Whenever we're working anywhere there could be ground-nesting birds, Ajax always has his muzzle on. When we're in the bush, the only time I take it off is if we've stopped for something to eat and drink. I often have my camera out then too, so that's why there are quite a lot of photos of him without it on. Sometimes when we're wandering along right up on the tops above the bushline, where there's no birds—hell, there's nothing up there for miles but tussock—I'll give Ajax a bit of a break from wearing his muzzle. No matter where we are though, if Ajax doesn't have his muzzle on, it's always close at hand so I can get it back on him quickly if I need to.

Once we're both geared up and ready to go, he'll usually take

Ajax with an adult female kea.

off ahead of me, turning back to make sure I'm still with him, but eventually he'll slow down a bit and wander along behind me. The reason for his changing pace is that a 'normal' day for us usually involves more than eight hours of going up and down hills looking for either birds or nests. I've got one of those step-counter apps on my phone and an average day is about 25,000 steps—and that doesn't take into account all the climbing and descending that we do. A mega day is anything more than 30,000 steps—that's when it starts to feel a little hard and when Ajax gets a bit tired.

A typical three-day trip will see me and Ajax cover about 60 kilometres on foot, crossing over mountain ranges, walking along rivers, shooting off up hills to check kea nests. On one of our mega days we might do about 35 kilometres on a track with a few diversions to check nests.

Our kea work usually runs from July or August until February or March, as it's focused on when the birds are nesting. Over that time, most of what me and Ajax do revolves around finding and monitoring kea nests.

The birds always nest below the tree line, but that can still be very high up in the hills. Their nests are usually in natural cavities, like rock crevices, hollows under tree roots, hollow logs, holes in tree trunks, under large boulders or dirt cavities under rocks. Often there'll be quite a long tunnel leading from the opening down to the actual nest.

Once an adult pair of kea have bonded and nested in a particular area, they don't tend to move far. Once we've seen them at a nest site, we know that they're likely to be in the near vicinity pretty much until they die. They seem to stay together year after year until one dies, then the other will re-pair.

They don't necessarily breed every year—every second year is more usual. When the pairs do breed, eggs get laid any time from July to January, with the peak time between August and October. Clutches can vary from two to five eggs, with four eggs being the most common. Each pair usually only produces one clutch per breeding season, but if a nest fails—the chicks die or get predated—

they have been known to re-nest. Some pairs will successfully breed twice in one season, although that is highly unusual.

In February 2017, I was out in Kahurangi National Park with Ajax and my partner Sarah checking nests. We were pretty deep in the park above the Wangapeka Track, and Sarah and I decided to split up and check two different nests, then go check some chicks at another nest. We were sitting up on the tops when I got a weird signal from a nest that we knew had already been predated and the chicks killed. The signal was telling me that the transmitter on this nest wasn't quite in nesting mode, but the output showed some very low activity that suggested the female had just laid an egg.

What we found really surprised me. The nest had a female sitting on a clutch of really young chicks. By that time of year, we'd expect the birds to be fully feathered, but these ones were really new. It's pretty unusual to see them nesting that late in the season. I kept an eye on that nest for a couple of months, and was pretty happy to see that the chicks not only survived nesting but also fledged successfully, even if they were a little bit late. It goes to show what good parents kea can be when they're left to get on with things.

The males are the ones who will pretty up the nest sites. They're fairly crude nests usually, but they'll bring sticks and chew them up to make a bit of a nest bowl with dried moss, some rotting wood and a bit of lichen. Nothing too fancy.

They'll do that with a few holes in the same area, then the females come in and have a bit of a look around, and choose the one they want to nest in. The birds clean out the holes and rebuild the nest every year. We've caught footage of them on cameras that have been left in place after the breeding season, and around April they'll come in and start mucking around with the nests.

Pairs will quite often have a network of holes, reasonably close together, but they tend to use the same ones year after year. If they're not in their usual hole and don't have a transmitter on them, it can be really hard to track them down. They could be 5 metres away or they could be 300 metres away, and there's no way to find out but to search every possible space. And I can tell you, when you start looking for random holes in the bush, there's heaps of them. If Ajax wasn't with me, I could be there for days and still not find them. But he'll head straight for the inhabited hole and signal to me that that's where the kea are.

If it's a bit later in the season and the chicks have started to explore the outside world a little bit, Ajax will also let me know where to find them. This is also something I probably wouldn't be able to do without him, as they can be pretty sneaky finding the spots to hide away in. Ajax just points to which direction they're in. Once I've reacted to his indication and have headed off in search of the birds, he'll sit down and quietly wait for me.

The eggs take a bit over three weeks to incubate. Once hatched, the chicks stay in the nest for three or four months. The female kea are the ones that do all the incubating, brooding and feeding, staying on the nest while the males go off to find food to bring back.

The feeding process is pretty simple—the male goes out and has a feed. Back at the nest, he regurgitates food for the female. The female then regurgitates the food again into the chicks' mouths.

If Ajax and I turn up while the females are still sitting on their eggs, the bird will barely react. It's hard to imagine a bird being so unafraid of any potential predator—let alone one the size of an adult human—climbing into their nest. But while kea were evolving, there were no predators for them to be afraid of, so they entirely lack that fear response. It's also why they don't freak out when they see Ajax. Most birds would be spun out by the presence of a dog, and either take off or try to scare him away. But usually kea will wander up and have a good look at him. The really brave ones will give him a bit of a peck, and the really, *really* brave ones have been known to try to nick a bit of fur out of his tail to take back to their nests!

When they've got big chicks and you're trying to get them out of their nests to place bands on their legs and take physical measurements, the mothers will sometimes get out of the way or head out the back door of the nest and not worry about the chicks. There is one adult female who is breeding now that gets pretty feisty with me and tries to bite me when I do this, but I think that

An adult male kea in
Nelson Lakes National Park.

could be because I banded her when she was a chick and maybe she remembers that.

The nests can be quite big and they get used year after year, so there can be a lot of poo stacked up in them. As you can imagine, it can get a bit smelly, which certainly helps Ajax to find them.

When Ajax finds a nest, he'll stand there in quite an awkward posture with his head on a weird angle, letting me know exactly where to look. If I do go to a kea nest and there's nothing there but he's still interested, he'll sniff the path of where the kea have walked recently.

A lot of the nest openings are big enough for me to crawl into, with a tunnel down to where the actual nest is. Some of them are quite roomy inside, even though they have only a small access hole. I've learned how to get into them without upsetting the birds too much.

After three months, any surviving chicks fledge, developing feathers and wing muscles that are strong enough for flight. I say surviving chicks because there's an average survival rate of 1.6 fledglings per nest in areas where there is pest control. The loss of eggs and chicks in unprotected areas is largely down to predation, and it has been found that only 1 per cent of nests are likely to survive during a year when there is a stoat plague.

Once the chicks have fledged, the parents carry on feeding them for another two or three months. This extra time they spend on and around their nests gives us more of an opportunity to track and monitor the birds.

Kea hang out with their parents for ages because there's so much they need to learn. They need to find out where all the food is and how to fly. When they're in the nest, they'll start getting their adult feathers, then they'll poke around outside a wee bit. They won't go too far away from the hole and they'll head back in pretty quickly.

Gradually, they'll start venturing further and further away outside. When they're out of the hole, they'll start flapping around to help build up their breast muscles to prepare them for learning to fly. As they get stronger, they'll start to jump off things around the nest to test out the whole flying thing. They're really vulnerable while they're in the nest, but they're even more vulnerable when they're learning to walk around and unable to fly.

Then they start wandering further uphill. As they reach higher altitude, they spend the nights in different holes or in a bit of scrub on the ground. They stick together as a family unit, with the adults coming and going while the young make their way up the hill.

Once they're just above the bushline, they'll find a high spot to jump off, and use the winds that whip up the hill to start learning to fly. The adults will sit up a bit higher, keeping an eye on the fledglings and, if need be, showing them what to do. That's the time of year when it's really good to go up to the mountain tops to catch them.

This is also the time when Ajax and I do the other main part of our work for the Kea Conservation Trust. As well as nest monitoring, we carry out population surveys. The survey is a way for us to find out how many birds are actually in each area, and what is happening to the population.

Actually, I say that Ajax and I are doing the work but mostly Ajax is only along for the ride. He'll scope out whether there are kea nests as we make our way up to the tops, and help me to check nests on our way home, but when we're doing the survey he mostly just sifts around keeping an eye on everyone but doing not much. That's because a lot of the time we know pretty much where the birds are going to be, and also because the birds are more mobile at this time so tracking them isn't as straightforward. Even though there's not much work for him during the actual survey, it's always handy to have Ajax there to sniff stuff out if we need him to—we do walk past a lot of nests and kea have been known to nest late in the season. It's really handy to have him there to confirm if there are kea anywhere below the bushline.

As the young birds are beginning to fledge, the birds will all be in a family group above where they've nested. If we're doing a survey in an area we've been monitoring, it's pretty easy to find the birds because they head straight up the hill from their nests. We'll camp just above the bush edge, where we'll have a good view of them either flying or hanging out. We'll make an assessment of how many fledglings there are compared to the number of eggs that were laid. Then we can catch the young birds, measure them, band them and, if need be, attach transmitters to them so we can track them. If we're working in an area that we haven't been monitoring during the nesting season, we head for the places where it is likely that kea will congregate.

To catch many bird species, you set up mist (very fine) nets and play recordings of their own calls back at them. They freak out and fly back and forth to find out where this bird is, and you can catch them in the net. Kea are the same—they'll come up close to you if you play their own call to them, but usually you don't even need to do that. You can use their inquisitiveness to help you.

While most birds take off if there's heaps of noise and activity, that's exactly what you need to attract a kea. If there's colour, sound and something going on, they won't be able to resist coming in to have a look. Then I'll be there waiting to trap them. It doesn't seem to faze them too much when I grab them, although I've got a few scars on my hands from ones that have decided to fight back.

We put two types of bands on every single bird we catch: a metal band with a unique combination of letters and numbers for identification, and a set of two plastic bands (one for each leg) with the same letter-and-colour combo. The plastic bands are produced in a variety of combinations, but there is only one of each set within a particular study area. So a bird in Fiordland and a bird in Arthur's Pass could have the same combo, but as they're not likely to be in the same place at the same time we won't get them confused.

Once we can get a good look at the bands, we are able to work out which bird we're looking at.

(If you see a band on a bird, take a photo if you can and note exactly where you've seen it. The more information you can collect at the time the better—location, time, date, what the kea was doing. If you send that info to the Kea Conservation Trust through its website, www.keaconservation.co.nz, it gets recorded into our Kea Database. If you find a band that's not on a bird, send it to DOC

National Banding Office, PO Box 108, Wellington 6140.)

We also measure the birds, take some blood samples and photograph them. The blood is collected for DNA analysis and lead sampling (kea are very susceptible to lead poisoning—see page 106). I have a portable testing machine that I take out with me, which takes about three minutes to give me results, to see whether the bird is being poisoned. It doesn't work in the cold, though—it's got to be warmer than 15 degrees, so that can make it a bit tricky in some places. When I first started using it, it was winter in Arthur's Pass, and I had to get the fire going and build up the temperature of the house before I could get it to work!

As well as all this, we put transmitters on females so we are able to track them to their nests in the future. We also put transmitters on the young birds. Then we can monitor if they survive, and if so, how far from the nest they go and where they settle. Kea are very robust birds and catching, banding and adding transmitters doesn't seem to bother them. They can go about all their natural behaviours unimpeded.

If we get dead signals from a transmitter, we can track the source and go out to retrieve the bird (or, in some happier cases, the dropped transmitter). This gives us a chance to analyse what has caused the bird's death. We've discovered that birds which are fed by people or which associate people with food are more at risk. That's partly because they're more likely to try to eat things that are toxic to them, but it's also because they are hit by cars, illegally shot or caught in traps set for other species.

My official role for the Kea Conservation Trust is as 'field co-ordinator'. I handle all the logistics for survey trips and liaise with all our people out in the field, as well as any volunteers who come out to help.

It is a real challenge to track wild kea, as the areas where we work are steep, thickly forested and often covered in snow (kea can start breeding while there is still snow on the ground). For the kea surveys,

An adult female kea checks out
Ajax as he takes a wee break.

we usually go into areas that we've been intensively monitoring for some time and try to spread the survey area out a bit further. Other times, we choose places where we know there are kea but they haven't been studied, and begin a completely new survey. With sites for new surveys, we need to make sure we are able to get there, get around the area and get back there in the future. There's not a lot of point in trying to monitor nests that are almost impossible to reach.

I do some of the planning using topographic maps. I'll look at the terrain, the contours, the rivers, the mountains, and think, *can I get through that piece of country?* I'll also look at how best to get in— will Ajax and I be able to make it in there on foot, or will we need a chopper or a boat to drop us off and pick us up? Are there good spots to camp and a water source close by?

The big multi-day trips take a while to plan, but for the shorter ones all I need to work out is how much food to take with me. I've pretty much got it down pat now. I know how much food I need, how much food I need to take for Ajax, what each of us likes to eat and what I can carry, so it doesn't take long to get organised. The night before we head out I'll spend about an hour making sure my bag's packed properly and going through a list of what I need. While I do that, Ajax usually just sits and watches. I reckon he knows that a trip is in the offing so he'll be a bit excited at the prospect of going out to work.

Heading out onto the tops, I have the usual massive pack that most trampers carry, but I'll also have all the gear that I need for catching and tracking kea, including camera equipment and large batteries. Ajax doesn't carry anything except for his hi-vis vest.

When Ajax finds a nest, I'll often set up trail cameras to help monitor the birds, so we can estimate survival rates and see how often the nest is visited by pests and whether it is being predated. Once we've set up monitoring at a nest, I aim to get back there within three weeks to replace the batteries, SD cards and memory cards in the cameras.

I put two cameras on each nest. One's on the outside, and is triggered every time there's movement, whether it's a kea or a goat or a stoat or a rat. That's to measure what's visiting. The second camera we put on the inside of the nest. It is also triggered by movement, and shuts off for 20 minutes after each photograph. If something moves again 20 minutes later, the camera will take another photo.

We use these to measure the survival of the nest. It's really hard to catch a predator in the act of attacking a nest—stoats are so quick and the cameras are designed for bigger animals, so you might not even get a photo of them at all. But using those images we're able to measure the length of the nesting period, and can tell how long the nest survives and whether it was successful or not (that is, whether any chicks have fledged).

Stoats are most likely to take eggs and kill chicks. The females are quite vulnerable when they're on the nest and stoats do kill adult birds but not that often, thankfully. Some females are stroppier than others!

It's really upsetting to see nests being predated. With all the time and effort we put in, having eggs or chicks killed by an introduced mammalian predator is devastating. All we can do is monitor the nests and hope that the birds make it. Once I banded a chick a few weeks before it was due to leave the nest. I showed up a couple of weeks later to collect the cameras, and there it was, dead.

Sometimes there's a good result, though. The other day Ajax took me to a nest that we'd been monitoring that had had two chicks in it. When we got there, the birds weren't there. But Ajax got a whiff of them and pointed to a secondary hole that we hadn't known was there. The sneaky kea had left their main nest and gone into this other hole. They had probably heard us coming and dived into the hole to hide from us. Without Ajax, I wouldn't have found them there and would have assumed that they were gone.

If we get to a nest and there's nothing there, I'll click my fingers to get Ajax to have a look. If once he's had a look I can see he's not remotely interested, that tells me the birds are long gone. I sometimes get him to check random holes where I think there could be nests— I'll click my fingers and he'll go and have a sniff, but if he shows no interest at all I'll know that they're empty.

There's a real difference in his body language when he's sniffing something else he's interested in that's not kea—like possums, goats or deer. I can read his postures, and they're really different for kea than for anything else. If anyone else went out with him, they probably wouldn't have a clue what he'd found or what he was sniffing out, but I've learned to read what my dog is thinking.

Early on, when I first started working with Ajax, when he would indicate next to a hole that looked like a kea nest I'd think, *sweet*— only to find that it was a possum. Eventually, I worked out that the way he was acting would be subtly different to the way he'd act if there were kea. Luckily possums are not very aggressive, so if I climbed into the nest to have a look they'd usually just hide as far back in the hole as they could. If possible, I take them out and kill them, but often they're just too hard to get out.

Ajax's nose for possums came in handy one night when we were setting up some traps at a friend's place. As we were wandered along, Ajax sniffed out certain trees and put his feet up on them. It was his way of showing that there were possums up in that tree. Everywhere he indicated, we put a trap down, and the next morning there was a possum in every one of the traps.

At least he knows that a possum is something he should be interested in, though. One night Ajax and I were staying out in a hut in the bush and there was a rat sitting outside, bold as anything. I looked at the rat, then looked at Ajax, but he was not remotely interested. I said, 'Get it!' Ajax still wasn't keen, but he wanted to keep me happy so he wandered up to this completely unafraid rat and gave it a half-hearted sniff before ambling off and sitting back down. In some ways, Ajax will always be that funny little puppy who was scared of a hedgehog! Mind you, in the bush there are so many rats that their scent is everywhere, so maybe Ajax just didn't think it was anything worth paying attention to.

KAHURANGI AND NELSON LAKES NATIONAL PARKS

A lot of people are surprised that I work with kea in the Nelson area—they seem to think that kea only live in the central parts of the Southern Alps and in Fiordland. Yes, kea live in the mountains, but they're definitely not just mountain parrots. They nest in the forest, so they have to come down from the snowline in order to breed.

I've seen them up in the hills near Collingwood, which isn't far from Farewell Spit. There's been reports of them around Cable Bay, a short way out of Nelson, and they live in the hills behind Kaiteriteri. Ajax and I live about an hour from Kahurangi National Park and 40 minutes from Nelson Lakes National Park, and both of these are home to plenty of kea.

Kahurangi became a national park in 1996, and it's this country's second largest, covering 452,000 hectares. It takes up a lot of the northwest corner of the South Island. You can probably get some idea of its size by the fact that you can get into the park from the inland town of Murchison, Karamea on the West Coast, Motueka in Tasman Bay and Tākaka in Golden Bay. Because the place is so big, there's a real variety of different landscapes in the park, ranging from high mountains right down to the sea. The West Coast is mostly podocarp forest, while beech becomes more predominant the further east you go.

Ajax and I spend a lot of time up on the tops, because that's where the kea tend to be, but to get there we have to traverse river valleys and climb up and down lots of hills. There are quite a few tramping tracks in the park, but we don't spend a lot of time on them. In the beech forest, the route that's easiest for us is wherever there is soft ground underfoot and a clear line of sight in front. The forest is pretty open underneath the canopy, so it's not like other parts of the country where animal tracks make for easier walking.

Because much of the park is limestone country, there's also an amazing range of cave systems, in which I've had some pretty cool adventures with Ajax. You wouldn't think a dog would be that into

Ajax goes caving in northwest Nelson.

heading underground, but I've taken him caving a fair bit and he's quite good at it. Because he's learned to be really tolerant of being manhandled when we're working, it's quite easy to lift him up rock faces or push him through holes when we're underground.

When I'm caving somewhere I've never been before, he's always able to scent the path back to the entrance, which is handy. Once when I took him into a new cave I reached what I thought was the end of the cave system. Ajax wasn't having it. He suddenly disappeared underneath a rock and didn't reappear. I followed him and crawled down where he was, only to find that there was a whole new set of caves underneath. That was a good find.

Another time I took him caving with some friends in a wet cave. He was really good for most of the way, but when we were halfway back he decided he didn't want to go much further. I encouraged him to keep going but I could see that he was getting a bit cold from being in the water. When we got to the end he was really reluctant to do the last swim. Eventually he got in and did it though.

We humans all took our wetsuits off and were getting our gear sorted when Ajax just stopped. He wouldn't get up and he wouldn't move. I hadn't realised how cold he was. I looked at his eyes and they weren't focusing properly. Shit, he had hypothermia! I hadn't ever thought about a dog getting that. I quickly dragged him out into the sunshine, dried him off with a towel and gave him a couple of One Square Meal bars. (I don't give usually give him human food, but it was all I had and there were good nutrients in it that I thought would be beneficial for any tired creature.) After a good feed and about half an hour in the sun, he was as right as rain. It gave me a hell of a fright, though, and it's made me really careful about making sure he doesn't get too cold now.

The other national park that Ajax and I spend quite a bit of time in is Nelson Lakes. While it's named after its lakes—the biggest ones being Rotoiti and Rotoroa—the park covers the northernmost ranges of the Southern Alps. It's a little over 101,000 hectares, and there's quite a bit of open tussock land up above the bushline.

Like the eastern side of Kahurangi, the forest here is beech.

Because the landscape here was created by glaciers, the valleys are really steep and often have scree-slope sides, which can be pretty challenging for me and Ajax to climb up on our hunt for kea.

The main DOC centre for the park is in St Arnaud on the shores of Lake Rotoiti. There's been a lot of work done in the area in terms of predator control, and they've managed to reduce the numbers of possums, stoats, ferrets, rats and cats to the point where they've been able to reintroduce kiwi into the park. Now that these birds are back, it's even more important for people to not take dogs into the park, as they are one of the main killers of kiwi. Most of the time Ajax is the only dog in the national park. Up the tops of the mountains, he'll mark his territory like the whole park is his!

This message is clearly getting out to people visiting Nelson Lakes, as I get some funny reactions from people who see me out there with Ajax. It usually doesn't take them long to work out that he's allowed to be there, but sometimes tourists get a bit scared of him. They see a dog with a muzzle on and think that he's a really dangerous dog. They'll jump out of his way, often with a bit of a squeal. At Nelson Lakes once, a woman panicked really badly. She ran off up the hill, shouting, 'Keep him away from me! Oh my giddy aunt!'

Poor Ajax sat there looking really confused. He really doesn't understand why anyone wouldn't like him.

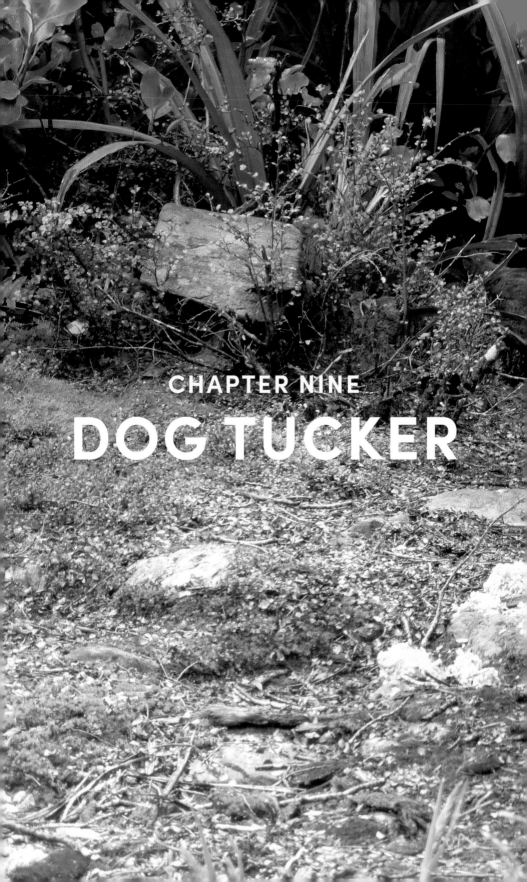

CHAPTER NINE
DOG TUCKER

Other dogs will hoover up anything you feed them, but not Ajax. He'll take his time to think about it and decide whether he's really that hungry first. At home, he gets a bit of competition from the weka, who will come and browse his food bowl and nick a few of his biscuits if he hasn't eaten them. Most dogs would lose it if they caught birds stealing their food, but not Ajax—he couldn't care less.

Quite often, I actually have to convince him to eat. I'll give him biscuits, and he'll look at me as if to say, 'Nahhh . . .' I'll be standing there saying, 'Just eat it!', and he'll be looking at me and looking back at the food, trying to decide whether he can be bothered eating. It's partly because he's not massively food-driven, but a bit of it is also because he wants something else other than biscuits. Quite often I'll give him biscuits in the morning and he won't eat them all day. They'll sit there until late afternoon when he's really hungry, then he'll scoff them down, not long before he gets his feed of meat for dinner.

In the evenings, as soon as I put my plate in the sink after I've finished dinner, Ajax will be up like a shot and waiting in the kitchen. He knows he gets fed after I do, but he'll always remind me, just in case I forget to feed him—which would be impossible!

What Ajax eats out in the field depends on how long we're away. If it's one night only, I'll take some dog roll for him, but any longer than that and I take dry biscuits, because they're lighter to carry.

While he's not too bothered about what he eats, I need to be careful to keep my food intake up. I take lots of chocolate and lots of lollies with me when I go out on a big mission. Carbs are always key too—lots of pasta and lots of rice. For three days, for example, I'll take some meat, lots of fresh veges and rice. Then I'll have a block of chocolate per day—always Whittaker's because they're the biggest blocks—and lots of muesli bars as well. I like having stuff I can eat while I'm on the move.

I'll just drink water from the streams. It's the best water out there—so much better than town water. I'd never drink anything around a farm or around one of the main tracks, because of the pooing habits of farm animals and tourists, but out where I'm working the stream water is absolutely beautiful.

Of course, Ajax drinks out of streams quite happily. Sometimes if we're in places where there's not a lot of water, I have to persuade him to drink from small ponds or big puddles. He's also learned that eating snow is a handy way of keeping hydrated!

If we're in limestone country during the summer, sometimes we don't find any water because it's all running underground. In those cases, I'll share the water I am carrying with him. That doesn't happen very often anymore, as the more time I spend out in that country, the better I've become at knowing where there's likely to be water—even a wee trickle is often enough to fill a bottle and to give Ajax a good drink. It might take me an hour to fill the bottle, but it's better than not having any water at all. I don't worry about taking filters with me as the water is so clean.

The worst thing that's likely to be in there is a bit of goat shit and that's nothing to worry about. I've learnt that most of New Zealand is pretty good for water, especially after spending time in Australia, where all the rivers seem to be full of salt. There seems to be more salt in the rivers than in the sea over there—that was weird.

I've got food stashes hidden in different places that I go back to regularly—and if I stash food for myself, I always hide some for Ajax as well. These stashes can be anywhere from in a hut, to in a bivvy, to under a big tree. Most of them are in places where other people don't tend to go, so I don't worry too much about them getting nicked. If anyone did find them I'd be quite impressed that

Ajax in the Marlborough Sounds.

they'd managed to get that far into the wilds!

On one work trip, I was taking a bunch of volunteers into the Kahurangi to help with a kea survey there. I had some dehydrated food in a big bin stored at a locked ranger's hut at the road end that I'd dropped off there the week before. We all stayed at the hut for the night, then in the morning I said to the others, 'All the food is in the big bin out the back. Tip it out and then help yourselves to what you need for the next ten days.' One of the guys opened it up, tipped the bin over and there was nothing there. The whole lot had been stolen. It was about $2000 worth of food and someone had flogged it.

I'd organised another volunteer trip that was due to go out directly after this one, so I had more food back at the office. I told the rest of the team that I'd jump in the truck and pick it up then carry it in, if they could take my stuff, including the dog food, between them. Everyone agreed, and they set off into the bush while Ajax and I headed back to the office to get the food. I needed to bring ten days' worth of food for about ten people, which even though it was dehydrated would be a pretty hefty amount for me to carry, but I figured it was the quickest way for us all to get where we needed to be.

After picking up the food, we made it back to the hut only to find that the volunteers hadn't taken all my stuff with them. It looked like a few people had taken a few bits, but bugger all of it was gone. I had no choice but to load it all up along with the food. My pack, with a big sack of dehydrated food strapped to the back of it, weighed about 40 kilos. Usually at the start of a trip I can lift my pack up and get it on my back no problems, as I'm really fresh (then, as the days wear on, it gets harder and harder to pick up). This time I couldn't put the pack on without sitting down and putting it up on a table. After a couple of tries I managed to hike it onto my back, but it was pretty uncomfortable. I was so annoyed.

It took me a bit longer than usual to hike up to where we'd arranged to meet, and Ajax was a bit confused about why we were going so slowly. By the time we got there I was absolutely knackered. I had all their food, but I soon found out that no one had bothered to bring the dog food up. Surely between them they could have put a little bit extra in each of their packs and it would have made hardly any difference to them! I was pretty disappointed in them all, so it wasn't a great start to the trip.

Luckily—for them and for Ajax—one of the places we were staying was near one of my food stashes. Thankfully, it hadn't been nicked and in there was a big bag of rice. I boiled up heaps of rice for Ajax and mixed it with Marmite, and that's what he ate. Lucky for him, he's very cute and a few of the volunteers felt a bit guilty, so his meals were often supplemented with leftover rehydrated human food. It was bloody tempting to tell them that they could all eat rice and Marmite while the dog ate their meals!

He obviously didn't hold a grudge against the volunteers though, as he was quite happy to sleep in their tents with them at night. Everybody wanted him to sleep in their tent because they reckoned he'd keep them warm, but it works both ways—they kept him warm too. Usually if I'm in the tent and it's cold outside he'll sleep at my feet, so he reckons it's a bit of a treat to snuggle up with other people.

A lot of times when we're out I'll shoot a goat and give some of the meat to Ajax, though I never rely on being able to find goats. The goat numbers in Kahurangi aren't too bad, and hunting is permitted out there, which helps manage the population. Their main impact is eating tree saplings, which means the bush takes ages to regenerate. If a big wind storm smashes all the big trees, there are no saplings to come through, so the bush takes so much longer to regrow.

If I get a goat, I'll give Ajax a leg and he's happy to have a bit of extra fresh meat in his diet—although I have to say I don't love his habit of eating half of the leg, then going off to bury the rest. That's all good until he digs it up again the next time we're in that spot. The meat can be pretty rank by then, but not as rank as Ajax's farts after he's eaten it. That's probably one of the main things he does that will get him kicked out of the tent at night!

Once I killed a goat and when we came back through that area about a month later Ajax managed to find the remains of the carcass and roll in it. Talk about sick-making—it absolutely stunk! I got him down to the river as fast as I could and pushed him in the water, and wouldn't let him out until he'd sloshed around for quite a while. Far out, that was gross.

That's not the grossest thing I've ever seen him do, though. One time, I had a Spanish volunteer from one of the zoos come out to see what we do. Most of the people who volunteer are either really keen on animals or really keen on the mountains. Sometimes they'll be people who work with kea as well. They're always eager to learn about the animal that they work with in captivity and to find out how they can enrich the lives of the birds they look after. It's great to have a chance to show them the birds in their natural habitat.

Tom, who works with me, picked this volunteer up from the airport and she stayed at his house that night. They had a nice venison stew for dinner, then the next day I took her out hunting for kea nests.

As we went along, I was telling her about the local sandflies, and how they can be pretty vicious out in the Kahurangi. She said, 'Have you got any bug roll?'

Thinking she was asking for insect repellent, I said, 'Oh, nah, I don't use that. I used to but I just don't bother with it anymore.' (By the way, my rationale for this is that sandflies are a bit like kea— they'll hang around where they think they'll get a feed. That's why there are swarms of them in carparks. When I'm out on the trail of kea I just don't stop moving, which makes it harder for the sandflies to get me. It takes a while for the carbon dioxide to build up around you so they can figure out where you are, so if you don't stop, they won't find you.)

She looked at me really confused and said, 'Ummm, OK . . .'

It took me a minute to click to what she was actually asking for. 'Did you mean *bog* roll?' I laughed awkwardly.

'Ah, yes . . .' came her reply, and she looked quite relieved that I wasn't some sort of weirdo.

'Oh, yeah, yeah, I've got some of that. Hang on a minute!' and I set about digging some toilet paper out of my bag.

She went off a discreet distance away and did what she needed to

Ajax at Kiwi Saddle Hut in Kahurangi National Park
with a group of our friends, colleagues and volunteers:
Tom Goodman, Phoebe van der Pol, Jimmy Sippo,
Liam Bolitho, Joel Zwartz and Leigh Marshall.

do, and then the two of us and the dog headed off up to the kea nest. Once we found it, I explained their nesting habits to her and showed her what we did to observe the birds.

On the way back to the truck, Ajax took off ahead of us. I figured he knew where he was going and let him run a bit. That was until I noticed that he'd headed off into the bush and he was clearly on the trail of something.

'Ohh, he's found something!' I shouted, thinking that he'd found a kea nest.

I raced off ahead, but once I reached him, my excitement quickly evaporated.

'Ohhhh, noooooo! Yuuuuuck!' There he was licking her poo! We'd failed to inform her of the bush etiquette of digging a little hole with the back of your boot, then kicking your shit into it and covering it over—and Ajax, who absolutely loves venison, was thoroughly enjoying the results. It was disgusting.

By this time, she'd caught up with me and was saying, 'What's he found? What's he found?'

Thankfully, I'd managed to quickly cover up the offending matter.

'Ummm, oh, nothing. Don't worry about it . . .' I replied, feeling myself redden as I quickly ushered her back down the track. To this day, she still doesn't know what happened out there, thank goodness.

CHAPTER TEN
JUST ANOTHER DAY AT THE OFFICE

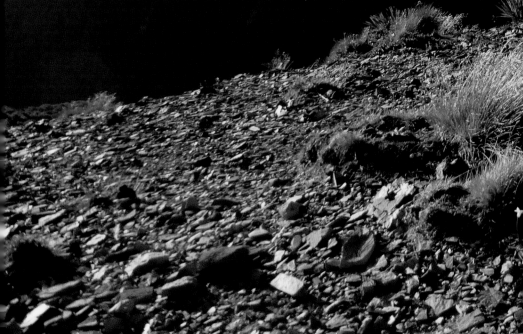

Ajax takes a ride in a helicopter.

What Ajax and I do is not like most jobs, purely because working out in the bush brings an unusual series of risks with it. We take every precaution to make sure that we're safe, but the environment that we work in is unpredictable. The weather can change—suddenly we can find ourselves in a blizzard or having to navigate an ice field. To do the work we do I have to accept that there's some danger.

The main reason I do it is because I am so passionate about the birds. Another reason is because it's awesome! I don't want to be stuck in an office and leading a mundane, predictable existence. For me, life's about excitement and new experiences, and I get that every day in my job. Some days more than others, though . . .

When we're working in quite remote spots, a lot of the time we'll get dropped off or picked up by helicopter. Thankfully, it didn't take Ajax long to get used to flying in style in the chopper. The first time I took him flying, I decided to treat it as if we were going for a ride in the car. I put him in the back seat of the chopper and tied him to my pack so he couldn't move around too much.

He sat there quite happily until we were in the air, then he freaked out a little bit. I think it was because of the noise more than anything—those machines are pretty loud when you're up in them. When I say 'freaked out', I mean he shuffled around a little, but he didn't bark or cry or anything. He probably would have been a bit more upset if he hadn't been able to see me and get some reassurance. Once he was used to it, he lay there quite happily. And after that first trip, he was as good as gold.

It didn't take him long to work out that all pilots are different and they have different rules when it comes to having dogs on board. The first few times he flew with a new pilot, they'd always insist that Ajax go in the pod, the bit on the outside of the chopper where any luggage gets stowed. To get him in that, I'd have to pick him up and squeeze his legs together so he couldn't splay them to stop me from putting him in there. Then I'd have to shut the lid of the pod on him. It was always quite an ordeal for me to get him into the pod, so you can imagine what it must have been like for him. He'd be stowed in there with the bags, which can't have been much fun for him.

Once he was in the pod with another dog, which took a bit of organising! To be fair, I don't know if I'd want to risk having two dogs that didn't know each other in the cabin of the chopper either.

Another time I'd shot a deer, and the pilot insisted that Ajax go in the pod with the carcase. He ended up sitting on the legs of the deer that I'd shot. That looked pretty classic. I'm amazed he didn't decide to have a feed while he was in there.

Ajax clearly doesn't like going in the pod, and he makes sure that I know it. He has worked out a scheme to try to avoid the pod altogether. As soon as the back door of the chopper opens, he is there like a flash and jumps in the back seat. It is like watching kids call shotgun on the front seat of a car. He learned that if he was quick enough, he might get away with staying in the back and avoid going in the pod.

Over the years, most of the pilots around our part of the country have got to know Ajax, and they're all pretty happy to let him inside now because they know how well behaved he is. He's so relaxed, he'll just sit there with his head against the window looking at the view. Some of the pilots bring him dog biscuits when they know they're picking us up. One pilot even lets him go in the front seat, which must look pretty hard-case when we come in to land. And it always makes me laugh how disappointed some pilots are if they arrive to pick me up and Ajax isn't with me. I've lost count of the number of times I've had a pilot greet me with the words, 'Where's your mate?'

Ajax likes to spend his time in the helicopter gazing out the window.

Quite often there are six of us in the back of the helicopter, with the packs stuffed in so that you can't even see the person next to you, and Ajax is jammed into whatever gap he can find. He'll sit there quite happily, because he knows the other option is being in the pod. It's the same in the back of the truck sometimes—all my gear will be in there and he'll squeeze in wherever he can fit. He's pretty happy just to be coming along for the ride.

That was certainly the case when a trip to the northern side of Mount Owen in Kahurangi National Park started off in spectacular fashion late one Friday afternoon. It had been raining a torrent of soul-piercing, frigid rain, the type that feels as though it has melted from snow only metres before it makes contact with the crown of your head.

We had been working around the Roaring Lion River for the previous two days and were awaiting pick-up by the local helicopter pilot. I was sure that due to the weather situation and the less-than-shining forecast that they would take us home, rather than heading to our next location, which was a nondescript knob in the middle of Kahurangi National Park. I was actually hoping that this would be the case and that before long Ajax and I would be enjoying the comfort of a hot meal and a warm, dry bed in my mate's house in nearby Karamea (although Ajax would be out the back on the verandah.)

The monotonous sound of falling rain was soon interrupted by the distant thump of helicopters blades reverberating across the vast valley system. Finally, the chopper was here to collect us from our makeshift camp.

As I began to load my saturated gear into the back of the chopper, I noticed that the equipment needed for the next portion of my work week was sitting there, ready to be unloaded at the next drop-off. I remember thinking that I didn't know why they'd bothered packing it, seeing as I was certain that the current weather conditions wouldn't allow for safe travel right across to the other side of the national park.

Reality began to set in when the pilot confirmed that we would indeed be heading to the next drop-off—a spot that had been unofficially named Miss Fire Knob. This meant that the helicopter would be dropping me there with my soaked-through clothes, my wet tent, my still-freezing core and my damp dog. Damn.

While Ajax sat looking out the window, I spent the rest of the flight mentally preparing for what I was going to do once I got to the drop-off point. Going through a gear evaluation in my mind, I determined that I had one pair of dry undies and a semi-dry bag. It was enough to get me through the night, although not in the most comfortable fashion.

We flew a direct path towards the Knob, with clouds, rain and wind impeding our progress the whole way. When we reached the final mountain range that we needed to get over, it was covered in a thick misty cloud, which was—to my relief—impenetrable in the eyes of our experienced chopper pilot. He turned the helicopter around and headed back to the coast, away from the angry weather plaguing Kahurangi National Park. I got that night in a warm bed in Karamea after all—and so did Ajax—and I was able to eat, sleep and dry all my gear ready for another attempt at getting into the mountains the next day.

The next attempt went a whole lot more smoothly. The sun was bouncing off the snowy mountain tops and we had an amazing flight through the national park. I saw things that I had never seen before, including vast amounts of deer sign—lots of footprints on a sandy bank and in a grassy clearing—that I marked in my GPS, determined to return there one day on foot, with a rifle in hand. Although probably not with Ajax as he is not the best deer-hunting dog.

(Once when Ajax was out tramping with me, I could tell I was on the scent of a deer. I could smell it, and then I found some deer shit that was still warm, so I knew the deer was nearby. Ajax had never been out deer hunting and had no idea what I was looking for. Just around the corner, I came across this deer standing there. Ajax was looking in the other direction. I loaded my gun and it jammed. I was so annoyed. I quickly tried to get the bullet into the shaft of the gun to load it before the dog saw the deer and chased it. Fortunately I managed to shoot the deer just as it ran off. It only made it about 5 metres before it dropped dead. All this time Ajax really had no idea what was going on. Even having seen me shoot and kill the deer, he didn't really get it. I can tell when he knows there are deer around, which helps me get ready to load, but he's no good at letting me know where they are.)

Anyway, back to the helicopter . . . It was an unceremonious drop-off on the top of the mountain. There were extensive valleys and vast peaks all around, as far as the eye could see. It was one of those days when I really loved my job.

As the helicopter flew off into the distance, Ajax and I made our way to the first kea nest we needed to check. There was a chance that it had eggs or chicks in it and that the mother was in there keeping them warm.

As luck would have it, this was exactly what we found: a female kea, which I had named Maiden on a previous trip, was sitting on some newly hatched chicks. They made themselves obvious with quiet squeaks of complaint as their mum adjusted her footing occasionally.

That was a good result, and then we were treated to a spectacular sunset, the mountains enveloped with a golden hue as the sun dropped below the horizon. I was completely in awe and felt really privileged that I was able to witness something so stunning.

The night was spent resting comfortably in my tent, silently spending the hours of darkness dreaming about what I had to do the next day. I awoke to find that dew had stealthily coated all of the bush we were about to walk through. It made for a cool start to the day, which got more damp as it went on.

We spent the day checking other kea nests and locating a transmitter that had fallen off a bird in the depths of one of the dark valleys that scatter the area. We made it back to camp as the sun was setting, this time without the spectacular display that I had been treated to only 24 hours before.

One of the things about working in the national park is that even when the weather's a bit cold, we move around so much that I'll

Ajax in the snow at Arthur's Pass National Park.

still find myself sweating my way up the mountainsides. It's only when I stop that I realise what the temperature actually is. That was certainly the case this night.

Having spent the day out in the wet bush, both Ajax and I were pretty damp. Once we got back to camp, I kept myself busy organising stuff for the next day and then cooking dinner. That kept me moving and kept me warm. It was only when I looked at Ajax that I realised how cold he was. He was shivering hard out; he must have been absolutely frozen.

I had to hop in the tent with him and put my sleeping bag over both of us. I ended up having to spoon him for about an hour to stop him from shivering! Once he was warm, I went out and cooked us both some dinner. He scoffed his down and I put him back in the sleeping bag while I set about preparing for a quick getaway the next day. While he made the most of being allowed in my bed, I ran outside, barefoot and in my undies, and gathered everything together so I wouldn't have much to organise when the sun returned in the morning. Then I quickly retreated to the warmth of the tent and my sleeping bag.

Before turning in for the night, snuggled up with Ajax, I checked the weather forecast. As is sometimes the case when you're out in the wilds, I felt like I had a better grip on what it was going to be like the next day than the forecaster did. They were saying it would be only rain that I would have to contend with; I was positive that there would be snow in the morning, and that there would be lots of it.

I woke up the next morning, feeling pretty happy that it hadn't rained or snowed, as I hadn't heard anything batter the tent during the night. As I opened the outer door of the tent I was shocked to be greeted by an icy blast. I stuck my head out and was greeted with a sea of white. There had clearly been an intense blizzard during the night, and snow was still falling softly but thickly.

It looked as though it was only going to get worse, so I decided to get dressed and get out of there. This proved to be easier said than done, as my wet pants and my damp boots had frozen solid overnight.

I had no choice but to put on these frozen pants and slam my feet into my boots to break the ice on them. I slowly packed everything up, then wrapped up the tent, which was pretty hard given the amount of ice on it.

Ajax was pretty reluctant to get out of the tent. He waited in there until I basically dismantled it around him, then at the last minute he came out into the weather and followed me down the hill.

I knew that getting back down to base was going to be hard. To get out of this area we would have to navigate down the mountain and traverse some dense forest canyons and steep river sides until we reached a poorly maintained track that would then take us over another mountain and eventually down the other side. It would have been a bit of a mission in good weather, so it was going to be a real trek in the freezing cold.

I put a thermal on Ajax to keep the biting wind off him. A lot of people reckon that a dog's fur is enough to keep them warm, but in extreme conditions like that, a smaller animal loses heat quicker than a human. That said, I wouldn't buy a special dog coat to keep him warm. He's got a high-vis vest, but if he needs an extra layer, I put some of my thermals or one of my jackets on him. It's multi-tasking—if I need it, it's for me, and if he needs it, it's for him. It means I don't have to carry extra gear when we're up in the mountains.

When I put a thermal on him, it fits around his chest but dangles down over his back end. If he cocks his leg to take a pee, sometimes he ends up peeing into it. When that happens, I'm like, 'Well, that's yours for this trip. I won't be fighting you for it!'

As we trudged along on our journey home we were constantly pelted with snow, with the snowflakes getting exponentially larger the more the altitude increased. At the highest point of the climb the snow was knee-deep in places, and because it was really fresh and soft it slowed me down considerably. Because Ajax is so light, sometimes he gets lucky and can scoot across the surface of the snow while I crunch along through it. This day, though, the snow was so fresh and light that he was sinking down into it alongside me.

Sliding down the other side of the mountain provided some fun for the day and had me wishing that I had my snowboard with me. As we got nearer to the road end, where the work truck was parked, the snow gave way to rain and the chill gave way to an uncomfortable dampness.

As soon as I got back to the truck, I ripped off my wet boots. That has to be one of the best feelings after a hard day in the mountains. But I was surprised to see a raw, bleeding blister on one foot— something I hadn't felt due to the numbness of the icy walk.

My other foot was even worse—there were signs of frostbite on the capillary bed underneath one of my toenails. That gave me a bit of a fright. Fortunately Ajax's feet were fine—he doesn't seem to have any problems with them in freezing conditions. It seems like dog's feet are much better adapted to rough conditions than those of us soft humans.

I didn't really think too much about my gross feet as Ajax and I both jumped into the truck. He usually travels in the back, but this day we were both so soaking wet and frozen I let him go on the floor in the front and cranked the heater up to full blast. I put one heater blowing straight in his direction and he stuck his head as close to it as he could. Meanwhile, I had the other heater blasting straight onto me. We were both pretty happy on that drive home.

When we got back home, I gave Ajax a big feed while I went off and had a hot bath to try to thaw out a bit more, then I ate pretty much everything I could get my hands on. It's amazing how being out in the cold makes us both really hungry.

The next day, after some good food and a long sleep, we'd both recovered from our ordeal, but I still had one little side-effect to remind me of it. A wee while later, the toenail that'd had frostbite under it started to fall off, but it was only loose on one side. I decided I needed to help it along, so I got out the pliers and tried to rip the rest off. It just wouldn't come out. Ho-ly! It was so painful. In the end I just hacked the whole nail down and let it grow back. It was pretty gross. But I still reckon what we do is better than any office job. And I reckon Ajax agrees with me.

Ajax on top of Woolshed Hill in
Arthur's Pass National Park.
This time it's covered in snow.

An adult female kea and chick in the Wairau Valley.

KEA INTELLIGENCE

A lot of people get to see kea only when the birds are investigating their belongings in high-country carparks. While that can be entertaining and/or exasperating, it also belies just how intelligent these birds are. Ajax and I get to see how smart kea are on a regular basis, but there's some interesting studies going on around the world that seek to prove what we already know.

It might seem like a strange place to be the forefront of kea research, but there's a captive population of kea in Vienna, Austria, that have been studied extensively. These birds are being taught to use a touch-screen computer to communicate, and are being studied to try to work out just how much kea understand when they copy human speech—they are parrots, after all!

There is also evidence that kea are able to make use of natural tools to gather food, although this seems to be more prevalent in captive populations than in the wild.

There was another study of kea done by researchers from the University of Auckland at Willowbank Wildlife Reserve in Christchurch. They gave the birds a test that had been given to other animals, including elephants and chimpanzees. The birds had to collaborate with one another in order to get food rewards, and this would take varying lengths of time. The results showed that the kea were able to wait longer than both the chimps and elephants to get their treats, meaning not only were they good at collaborating but they can show good self-control—when they want to!

That self-control isn't always evident, especially when there's something to play with. Even then, the play often requires collaboration. There have been several recent examples that show how smart and curious kea are.

In late 2016, a group of kea were captured on film moving road cones around in an area of roadworks near the Homer Tunnel on the road to Milford Sound. This was discovered after road workers kept arriving to find that the cones had been dragged out of the tunnel and left in strange places. Eventually, a 'kea gym' was built to keep the birds entertained and prevent them from hanging out on the road, where they could be at risk of getting run over.

Similar playgrounds—consisting of metal frames with stuff that will interest kea hung on them—have been installed by the Kea Conservation Trust in Arthur's Pass, Nelson Lakes National Park and Motueka. The Arthur's Pass playground was designed to try to lower the death rate of the birds in the area, caused by them being shot or trapped (both of which are highly illegal), eating rubber from cars or lead from nails and roof flashings, or getting killed while trying to car-surf their way down the Ōtira Gorge . . . teenage kea and teenage humans seem to have a bit in common there.

Speaking of Arthur's Pass, we got to see kea exploring and exploiting there at close range one day when we sat down to eat our lunch. My partner Sarah put her sandwich down on the seat for two seconds and it was gone. The sandwich was unopened in one of those sealed triangular plastic containers, but the bird simply knocked it off the seat, flipped the container open and took off with her sandwich. It just goes to show that they can pull their tricks even on people who really should know better!

An adult female keeps an eye on her chicks in Nelson Lakes National Park.

CHAPTER ELEVEN

THE RISKS OF THE JOB

Ajax and I have had our fair share of scrapes over the years when we've been out working. For pain, though, I reckon the worst thing was getting a bit of speargrass up my fingernail. It got embedded up to about midway up my nail. To get it out, I had to get a needle and stab it up the side of the speargrass then sort of scrape it out. Shit, that hurt!

I'm pretty good at treating any minor injuries in the field myself, but there was one time I had to get stitches. I'd been tracking a transmitter that had fallen off a bird. Just after I'd managed to find it, I was coming down the hill and scratched my leg on a bit of bush. It's a pretty common risk of the job so I didn't think much of it—until I looked down. The branch had scratched the whole length of my leg, but then I saw that a stick had stabbed right into the flesh—and broken right off. There was a chunk of stick stuck right into my leg.

I got my pliers and pulled it out, but I could see there were heaps of rotten bits of stick still in the wound. I had to go to hospital, and they cleaned it all out then stitched it up for me. There were still a few bits of wood that got left in it and it took a while for them to work their way back out. That was pretty nasty.

Ajax has had a bit of a rough time out there, too. Once we were out checking nests and he started whining. I thought, *what's going on here?*, because he's usually so chilled out. He seemed to be stuck to the ground, and couldn't move.

Ajax has dewclaws on the inside of his front legs, which not all dogs have. They're basically an extra claw that's higher up on a dog's foot than its other claws. They don't touch the ground—they're sort of like the dog version of a thumb.

A sapling had gone through his dewclaw and he couldn't pull his foot away. It must have been so painful for him. I had a good look at it and realised that the only thing I could do was pull out the piece of wood. He didn't look happy about it but was very glad to be released from the sapling.

He's also been stung by wasps a few times. The first time that happened, he had no idea what was going on. I tried to see if the wasp was still attached so I could flick it away, but he must have thought that it was me causing the pain so he tried to bite me!

From about January onwards, I get stung most days. There are wasp nests everywhere—the whole forest is humming with them, it's crazy. The impact of the infestation of wasps is huge. They hassle everything within their radius. If you get within 15 metres of a wasp nest, you'll get stung. There's no avoiding it.

Quite often, when we're out, Ajax will be out in front of me so it's he who will disturb the nest. Then the wasps will all start shooting out like missiles hunting down whatever has disturbed them. Usually it's the second person along that gets stung—and that's me.

I have got quite good at avoiding them by working out where the nests are likely to be, but sometimes it's impossible to move fast enough to avoid them. Down in the beech forest, the biomass of wasps is phenomenal and greatly outweighs that of most other creatures in the forest.

They have absolutely no useful role in the ecosystem at all. They're just pests and parasites. They steal off bees, they kill flies, they are a complete nuisance. There's some research being done into a mite that could potentially control wasp populations, which would be fantastic if it works. There's some wasp control done by laying baits, but that's pretty intensive work given how prevalent they are in the beech forest.

In my view, if there's any introduced pest that would be a good candidate for genetic control, it would be wasps. Their genetic diversity is very low, so if it was possible to figure out a way to manipulate that to help wipe them out here, I think it would be a really positive thing.

Another time when Ajax could have got quite badly injured, he was off on the scent of a kea and must have wandered into an area where there were kārearea (New Zealand falcons) nesting. These birds are highly territorial and will go to pretty much any lengths to protect their nests. Needless to say, they didn't take too kindly to having a furry, four-legged invader in their territory.

Ajax had his head down and was fully engrossed in the hunt for kea when they made a couple of close swoops to try to get him to change his route. It got them precisely no reaction from the dog at all. He had a job to do and nothing was going to distract him; besides which, he just doesn't see birds as any kind of threat. He probably didn't realise that these ones could have inflicted quite a bit of damage if they'd wanted to.

They came around and had another go, this time closer in. Still nothing. Not a flicker of an eyelid or a lift of the head. After another divebombing attempt, which still got them no reaction, the birds must have realised he wasn't interested in them or their eggs or chicks. Given how badly injured some people have been by divebombing falcons, it was amazing that Ajax got away with his skin intact.

While Ajax ignores most things, he's pretty alert when it comes to pigs, and that nearly got us in trouble one day out in the Kahurangi. We'd been checking kea nests and were heading back down to where the truck was parked. I'd just stopped for lunch when Ajax started barking. I looked around to find out what had got his attention and could see he was barking at a pig. It was sitting there looking at him and he was barking away.

It was not long until Christmas, so I figured I could go get it and that would be Christmas dinner sorted. I grabbed my knife out of my bag and walked up towards the pig. The closer I got, the more it dawned on me how big this pig was. It turned out to be a great big boar that had been living in the area for years. I'd seen its tracks a heap of times but had never actually come across it. It was *big*. And my knife was tiny.

Ajax was barking away at the pig, and the pig was looking at me, and I was looking at the pig. Then the pig shot across and started chasing the dog. Ajax sprung up onto a dead tree and leapt off it into thin air on the other side to get away from the pig. With the dog out of its sights, the pig turned around and started chasing me.

I ran around the tree just as the dog came back around to have another bark at the pig. It stood its ground and looked at the pair of us. I could see its eyes as it was trying to decide what to do. I knew this could go one of two ways.

The pig stared at us as we stared back. Then it looked us up and down, turned around and sauntered off really slowly, as if to say, 'Nah, can't be bothered today. But I definitely won this one.' Needless to say, we had turkey for Christmas lunch that year!

Pigs don't cause too many problems in the park—they're not hard-wired predators, so most of the risk they pose is ripping up nests by accident when they are rooting around in the ground. In terms of native species, the thing they are the biggest threat to in Kahurangi are the giant nocturnal *Powelliphanta* snails. More species of these huge snails are found in Kahurangi than anywhere else. The biggest ones—*Powelliphanta superba prouseorum*—can measure as much as 10 centimetres across and weigh 90 grams, which is the same as a fully grown tūī.

Being so big and meaty means the snails are a favourite snack for both pigs and possums. These days it is rare to see one of these big old snails out in the wild, but left alone they can live as long as 20 years. The impact of predation by pigs and possums has been so great that it's not known how many of these amazing snails survive, or indeed whether pest control in the region will be too little, too late. I really hope not, as they're very cool creatures.

There's one native species that Ajax and I don't love, and that's the lowly biddy-bid (the name comes from a mishearing of the Māori word 'piripiri', meaning to stick or cling). At the start of each year, there's biddy-bids all around. These annoying little plants are officially called *Acaena novae-zelandiae*, and they're New Zealand's tiny bit of revenge on the world for sending us heaps of pest plants and predatory creatures. *Acaena* species have been declared noxious weeds in some other parts of the world, and they annoy gardeners and outdoorspeople in both the United States and the United Kingdom.

The plants themselves can grow to be absolutely huge—like 4 or 5 metres wide—but it's not the plant itself that's so annoying. It's the little seed head that develops after it's flowered that causes the problems. These things are covered in little barbs—all you need to do is brush past them and your socks, trousers, hair, wool or fur will be absolutely covered in the little buggers.

I get them in my socks a lot, but it's OK for me as I can just chuck them in the wash and that gets rid of them. It's not quite so straightforward for Ajax. His whole body gets covered with them because he's got such long fur. They get in his ears, his tail, everywhere. If he gets the chance, he'll jump in the water and have a bit of a swim, which seems to get a lot of them out. Sometimes I see them all matted up in his fur and I think, *this isn't going to end well*, but he'll do a bit of grooming of an evening and pull them out with his teeth.

Sometimes he'll miss a few and they'll make his fur like dreadlocks, but the seed heads have evolved to fall apart eventually so that the seeds can spread, so either he gets them or nature takes its course. Every now and then I have to give him a bit of a helping hand if they get too deep in his coat, and cut them out. He's not a big fan of that, but he's always happy when they're gone.

Part of the reason he doesn't like me cutting out the biddy-bids is probably due to the fact that I once tried to give him a haircut when I thought he was getting too hot in the summer. I used a pair of scissors and got stuck into his fur, but it was too hard because there was so much of it. I couldn't get it even, so he ended up looking diseased for ages. I cut his back half and it looked really bad so I gave up on the rest. He was embarrassed for a wee while until it grew back. I have thought about shaving him but leaving a wee mane so

Ajax crosses a stream in the Wairau Valley.

he looks like a lion—that would freak people out when I'm out in the bush with him. But he's such a good-looking dog I don't want to embarrass him too much!

Biddy-bids aren't the most annoying plant, though. The worst plant is ongaonga, the native tree nettle. Its scientific name is *Urtica ferox*—which is Latin for 'to burn fiercely'. That about sums it up. They're one of the most poisonous plants in this country. The plants can get up to 2 or 3 metres tall with a diameter of about 12 centimetres, but they'll grow together in big thickets, which can be quite tough to make your way through. They grow all over the North Island and as far south as Otago, mostly found on the fringes of lowland and coastal bush.

When you touch it, you know about it. The leaves look a lot like normal stinging nettles but the hairs on them are like wee needles that are full of poison. When you brush against them, they inject toxins into your tissues.

As much as I hate it, I'm lucky that it doesn't affect me that badly. Some people get a very red, sore, itchy rash, but after touching it, my skin just really stings. Then every time I touch water for about a week afterwards that tingle comes back—water definitely makes it heaps worse for some reason.

It's surprising that ongaonga is not more well known, given how nasty it can be, especially if you stumble into it unsuspectingly. I've had a few rough encounters with it. I'd rather be stung by a wasp than ongaonga—but obviously not more than one wasp!

I've read about dogs that have got caught up in it and the poison has really affected their brains, or even worse cases where they've been unable to breathe, had convulsions and died. Thankfully, Ajax seems to be OK with it. He might have had the odd whack to the nose from it, but he doesn't avoid it. It doesn't seem to bother him. He avoids bush lawyer and speargrass, though. He obviously associates those with being annoying and he'll go out of his way to go around them. But I guess he's never had a real bad face-full of ongaonga.

One of the reasons he avoids ongaonga is probably because I'm quite wary of it. If Ajax sees me doing something, he likes to try to do the same thing. Sometimes that's not the best plan of action for him, though. There have been a couple of times when it's nearly ended in tears—for both of us.

One time we'd spent the day checking on kea nests in Arthur's Pass National Park and were coming down Kellys Creek, just out of Ōtira. It was a pretty steep descent and, like most of the creek beds in the area, this one was full of rocks. We got to a spot where there was no choice but to slide down quite a steep slope covered in loose stones. I decided I'd get Ajax to wait on a rock at the top while I slid down the hill on my arse. My plan was that once I'd got down safely, I'd get him to come down and I'd catch him at the bottom.

Plan in place, I sat him down, gave him the command to stay and headed off, slipping and sliding down the hill. A few seconds later, I heard rocks moving above me. It seemed that Ajax had decided that if it was good enough for me to slide down the hill then he was going to do it too. To start with, he was sliding down head first, but as he gathered momentum and got closer to me, he lost control and his back end swung around. Before I could get out of the way, Ajax hit me broadside and landed right on top of me. He looked a bit surprised to find himself there. Luckily for him, I was quite winded so couldn't even muster the breath to tell him off for not staying put when I told him to!

A similar thing happened at the start of 2017, when we were doing some work in Wānaka. It was the middle of summer but there was a big patch of snow on the south side of a mountain up above the Mātukituki Valley. I looked at it and decided it would be a quick way to get down—I reckoned I could sort of ski down it in my boots.

I jumped onto it, only to find it was solid ice. I just slid off down the hill. I tried to dig in my boots to help me slow down but it made no difference. I chucked my hands out behind me to see whether they'd help slow the slide, but that didn't help much. At the bottom I managed to kick out into the scree at the end of the patch of ice and lay there, happy to have finally stopped.

And then I looked up. There was Ajax flying down the ice behind me. He didn't even stop to think about it—as soon as I jumped he

Ajax has a cuddle with volunteer Rosie Willacy in Kahurangi National Park.

followed me. He was making the weirdest noise, a sort of unhappy whimper, as he skidded out of control down the hill. Then, seconds later, he slammed right into the back of me. It was a great way to get down the hill nice and fast, even if it wasn't quite what either of us had expected!

CHAPTER TWELVE

AJAX GOES ON HOLIDAY

Our kea work usually runs from July or August until February or March, focused on when the birds are nesting. I don't have much to do for the Kea Conservation Trust over winter so I usually take some time off, go somewhere warm and do conservation work there. While I'm away, Ajax gets to go on holiday as well. We both have very different sorts of adventures when we're away from home.

Although I spend so much time in the mountains, I don't like how cold it gets here over the winter. As a result, I've spent time volunteering in Australia, Europe, Africa, Central America and North America during our winters. Most of the work has been around birds, but in Australia and Africa I've done mammal work. Between 2010 and 2018, I've only had two winters in New Zealand.

For example, last winter, Sarah and I spent time on Christmas Island, northwest of Australia, then on some islands to the south of Western Australia. Christmas Island was unique—there were heaps of red crabs everywhere, which migrate from the land to the ocean to lay their eggs. The whole island is overrun with them. A few weeks after they lay their eggs, all the baby crabs come back onto the island—there's millions of them making their way up the beaches. It was amazing.

In Western Australia I did some work on catching feral cats, putting collars on them to work out where they went and what the best way was to kill them. When I was heading over there I put a post on Facebook to let people know what I was off to do. I got some really bad feedback from that—one of my relatives told me it was really terrible and that I shouldn't even say things like that, much less do them. I replied saying that I was really proud of what I was doing and that it was all about helping native species and the environment.

It's really hard to get some people to understand about predators and predation. It's hard-wired into those animals—cats, ferrets, stoats, rats and possums—to kill because they can, not because they need to eat. In New Zealand, the only real way we have to protect our birds for the future is by killing the creatures that predate them. Some people find this reality unpalatable and accuse people who engage in pest control of hating animals. That couldn't be further from the truth—I have loved animals all my life. But for the conservation of New Zealand species, I can see that these particular animals don't belong here and we need to get rid of them.

All the times I've been away for winter, I've always had someone to look after Ajax. Quite often, people will offer to look after him—some of my friends can be a bit competitive about who gets to have him, which is pretty funny.

Whenever I come back from being away—especially if I've been away working all winter—Ajax is thoroughly excited to see me. He runs around in circles like a mad thing, his tail wagging dangerously fast while he barks happily. I love sneaking up on him when I get back. I'll wait until his back's turned and then walk around the corner. He usually does a bit of a double take when he sees me—he'll look around, then go back to what he's doing, before turning back around when he realises it's me. That's when he really goes nuts. It's one of the best feelings to see him so happy to see me.

Every time I come back from being away over winter, he is always heavier and a bit out of condition. No one looking after him can keep up with the sort of mileage that we do when we are working and the sort of country we do it in when they're just walking him around the local park and playing Frisbee in the back yard!

The first year I had Ajax, my mum looked after him over winter. She ended up having a lot of run-ins with the neighbours and heaps of drama because of him.

When people meet Ajax now they notice how cruisy he is, but he certainly wasn't like that when he was little. Ajax was about nine months old when I asked Mum if she and her husband Ray could look after him for three months while I went to Australia to do some volunteer research with parrots and the Gilbert's potoroo, which is the world's rarest marsupial. It's so rare that it was believed to have been extinct until some were found in a nature reserve in Western Australia in 1994. There's only about 70 left and they live in an area of less than 1000 hectares.

They agreed to look after Ajax while I was away, and Mum reckons that they counted down every single one of those 90 days! To start with, when Ajax first arrived at their house their cat wasn't happy at all. Even now when he goes to visit them their cat will hiss and carry on, but Ajax completely ignores him.

The first day Ajax was staying with them, Mum got home from work and Ray said, 'You'll never believe what's been happening!' Mum almost didn't want to hear what he was going to say, and it was much worse than she was expecting.

Ray launched into the first of many stories of Ajax's exploits. This day, Ajax had jumped over the gate, gone up the road and joined forces with the neighbour's dog, Odie. Together, they disappeared up to the farm at the end of the road. There the two of them got in the shed amongst all the sheep's dags and made a hell of a mess. The farmer, who Mum and Ray knew really well, came down and said to Ray, 'If I ever catch that dog at my place again, I'm going to shoot it!'

Mum told me that she was so upset, she was almost in tears—not because she'd formed a bond with Ajax, but for my sake. She really didn't want to have to tell me that my dog had been shot! She went off down the road to see Victor, the farmer, and tearfully told him, 'You can't shoot my son's dog!' He said, 'I can and I will!' That failed to put her mind at ease.

Every morning before work, Mum goes for a walk. The day

Me and Ajax on a glorious day in Kahurangi National Park. PHOTO BY ANNE BAUMUNK

after her run-in with Victor, she went out for her walk, and within minutes she could feel this strange vibration in the footpath. Before she even had a chance to think about what it was, there was Ajax, bounding along next to her. He'd jumped over the gate and come running down the road after her. It made her even more worried about him going back to the farm and getting himself shot.

Luckily for Ajax, Mum talked to a friend of hers who'd had quite a few issues with her dog. She suggested that Mum talk to a local lady, Sarah Hesketh, who was renowned as a bit of a dog whisperer. Desperate to do something to stop Ajax from getting in more trouble, Mum called Sarah and she agreed to meet Ajax.

Sarah said to Mum, 'You realise that having a dog of that age and that breed is like having a teenager come and live in your house. You've got to treat him accordingly.'

She recommended that Mum shut Ajax in the conservatory out the back of the house. She assured her that it wasn't an awful thing to do to him, because he would be happy to be inside. If she left him outside, he'd roam around looking for mischief, which was obvious from the fact that he'd only been there a few days and had already dug a whole lot of holes in the lawn and the vegetable garden. He needed to be contained when Mum and Ray weren't around, and he had to know that they were in charge.

When he was in the conservatory, he was absolutely fine. They'd leave him in there overnight, and in the morning when they'd go out to the kitchen Ajax would be standing upright on his hind legs, looking at them through the window with his doleful eyes as if to say, 'Please let me out. I need to go to the toilet.'

It was still tricky when they'd try to take him out for walks, though. Ray took him out one day and Ajax was so used to being able to run free that he pulled Ray along the whole way. He wasn't used to being on a lead, so he'd take off, dragging Ray behind him.

It was a challenging three months for them to say the least. It probably didn't help much that I went home for a couple of days in the middle. Ajax was so happy to see me that he followed me around the whole time I was there.

Mum reckoned that after I left, Ajax went to the gate and stood on his hind legs and howled for about ten minutes. She said it was really heart-wrenching to hear Ajax crying so much.

One of my mates told me that he'd been doing some roadworks up the road and Ajax wandered past by himself. My mate was like, 'I'm pretty sure that's Corey's dog . . .' He went and grabbed the wandering dog and took him back to Mum's. Poor Mum apparently looked a bit confused, because she thought he was still in the back yard. But no, his curiosity had got the better of him once again.

I think that Ajax saw Mum as a bit of a replacement for me when I wasn't there. He'd come bounding out to the gate when she got home from work, keen to find out where she'd been and what she had with her. Mum said she felt a bit like he was picking on her, but he just wanted to be near her. They still have a really close bond—Ajax loves going to stay with her now, and he's much better behaved.

Although she never said it at the time, Mum was pretty sceptical about whether I'd be able to train Ajax to work with me. To be fair, if he carried on with me the way he did with Mum, I'd have had my doubts, too.

When I got back from Australia, she told me that he was the worst-behaved dog she'd ever come across. It makes me laugh, because now everyone else says he's one of the best-behaved dogs they've ever met. I reckon it's because she's not very authoritative with him, so he sees her purely as someone who feeds him. He'll do naughty stuff and she'll wave the newspaper at him and say, 'Ohh, get down, you naughty boy!', whereas I'd whistle and really growl him.

It was a bit scary for Mum to think that my dog might end up getting shot while I was away. One time when I'd been out mountain-biking I saw a dog ripping a sheep's face off so I can understand why the farmer reacted like he did, but I'm very glad Ajax didn't get caught down at the farm again.

Quite often when I'm away, Ajax goes to stay with my friend Jarrod and his wife Cherie in Christchurch. A couple of years ago, he stayed with them while I was doing some volunteer work with parrots on an island in the Caribbean.

Ajax with his pal Dusky,
hanging around camp in
Kahurangi National Park.

I didn't have internet coverage where I was working, but every now and then I'd head into the nearest town. When I got back into mobile reception after quite a while in the backblocks, I got a message from Jarrod. He said that Ajax was at the emergency vet's because he'd been pissing blood.

The message had been sent a few days earlier. I was about to call but realised it was the middle of the night back in New Zealand, so I sent him a message asking what was wrong. I had to wait until the next day to get a reply. Man, I felt absolutely stink.

The following morning I had a reply from Jarrod explaining what had happened. The vet had X-rayed him, scanned him, given him some antibiotics and put him in a kennel. That's the worst thing that could have happened to Ajax, because he's not used to being cooped up in a kennel, and he's never really been left alone, so that would make him all sad and mopey. The stress of the whole situation definitely wouldn't have helped him to recover. Luckily, he came right, though they never worked out what was wrong with him.

If the same thing had happened when Ajax was with me, I might have given him a day to see what happened, and just kept an eye on him. Knowing Ajax, it would have been caused by him eating something rotten, or it could have been an infection. I guess because Jarrod was in charge, he was worried about Ajax dying while I was away, so he rushed him to the vet on a Saturday.

Jarrod works in construction and he'd taken Ajax to work with him. All his workmates loved having the dog on-site. I reckon he must have dug up and eaten something that messed with his kidneys or his bladder, and he'd had a bad reaction to it. Eventually it would have flushed through his system.

Jarrod covered all the bills until I got home, and when we added it all up I ended up paying $2500! I had absolutely no regrets about paying, though, because I'd much rather have Ajax with me than not.

It's a miracle that Jarrod still offers to look after Ajax, as the dog always seems to disgrace himself when he's in Christchurch. Once when I was away, Jarrod took Ajax to work with him and left him in the car while he took a work truck to the dump to drop off some rubbish. When he got back one of his workmates said, 'Mate, your dog was whining real bad at the window for ages. But he's stopped now so he must be OK.'

Jarrod walked over to his car to find something that resembled a scene from a horror movie. Poor Ajax had obviously eaten something that didn't agree with him and he'd needed to get it out—fast. The inside of Jarrod's car looked like a Jackson Pollock painting. There was runny dog shit all over the windscreen, the steering wheel, the front seats . . . everywhere. Apparently, Ajax looked really guilty and sorry for himself—but not as sorry as I imagine Jarrod looked.

A couple of years ago, when I had a wedding to go to, I left Ajax with Cherie. Ajax sees Jarrod as the boss when I'm not there, and usually he's really good with him and will stay put. This time Jarrod was away with me, and Cherie put the dog in an enclosure that Jarrod had specially built for him. Then Cherie went out, thinking Ajax would be as good as gold while she was gone.

Not one to enjoy being left to his own devices, Ajax climbed out over the wall and took off. The next thing you know, while I was on the beers at this wedding, I get a phone call from the local council saying that Ajax had turned up at someone's house.

I called Cherie and told her that Ajax was up the road. She went off and picked him up and took him back to their place, and I went back to the wedding celebrations.

Jarrod and Cherie live on a fairly busy road in Templeton, on the main route south just out of Christchurch. Two days later, Ajax decided to bugger off again. He has very little experience in avoiding traffic, and when Cherie called me to say he had gone missing again, I was absolutely convinced that he'd be dead, run over by a car or a truck. But no—he was away for the whole day, then turned up back at their house right on dinner time. I still have no idea where he went or how he survived the traffic, but I reckon he was probably out trying to find me.

I've done my best to teach Ajax about roads, but as we live out in the country and work in the bush, he hasn't had that much experience of cars. That road south out of Christchurch is impossible to cross even when you know what you're doing—I hate to think how he managed it.

A similar thing happened when I was in Auckland one time. I got a phone call from the council in Nelson, and they said, 'Are you in Auckland?'

'Ummm . . . yes?'

'Is your dog with you?'

'Ummm . . . yes?'

'Ah, OK—he's at this address. Can you go and pick him up?'

I was having a group meeting with some university students who were doing a project about kea and had to say to them, 'I've got to go. My dog's run away!' Then I took off back to my mate's place on the North Shore, where I was staying. A few minutes later, I got another call from the same lady at the council in Nelson.

'Your dog's not there anymore. He's now at this address . . .'

He had been locked in the back yard at my mate's place, and it had a 1.8-metre-high fence. It never occurred to me that he'd be able to get out.

I went to the second address I'd been given and knocked on the door. I was a bit surprised when the lady who lived there invited me in. I walked in to find Ajax lying in the middle of the floor with a bunch of kids patting him and making a big fuss. You'd have thought he lived there!

The next day, he did it again—jumped the fence and disappeared. I knew exactly where he'd be, so I walked up the road and knocked on the door. Sure enough, there he was being treated like a king by the kids!

Once I'd managed to tear him away from his new fan club, I gave him a bit of a growling, then decided to try to work out how the hell he got out. I made sure all the gates were shut, then went around to the other side of the fence and called him. As soon as I said, 'Come here!', he went barrelling at the fence, jumped up, grabbed on to the top of the fence, then pulled himself over. I was absolutely amazed at how easy it was for him to climb this 1.8-metre fence. Maybe Mum was right when she said he was the naughtiest dog in the world . . .

CHAPTER THIRTEEN

A NEW JOB FOR AJAX?

Ajax is definitely slowing down.
He is resting here beneath a tree
in Kahurangi National Park.

Over the last wee while, Ajax has started to slow down a bit. He's getting older—he'll be seven in September 2018—and he doesn't have the stamina he used to have to go on big missions as often. Part of that is because each time I come back after winter, he's put on some weight, so it's harder on his body when he gets back out into bush at the start of the season. He loses weight and gets fit again quite quickly once we get going, but it takes him a while. Now I try to take him out on shorter trips early in the season and that seems to help get him back into condition.

I've also noticed that he's not quite as agile as he used to be, and his joints seem to be getting a bit sore. I've been trialling him on some anti-inflammatories to ease the discomfort. They seem to have been working but they're not going to fix him completely. He isn't really up to the big multi-day trips anymore, so I have to be much more careful about planning how long he is out in the field with me.

Not long into last season, I took him out on a big day-trip as a tester to see how well the anti-inflammatories were working. We'd had a big day, going up and down, and were at the top of a hill, just about to come back down. There were only another 5 kilometres to go, but Ajax decided he'd had enough. He sat down and absolutely refused to move.

I did everything I could to persuade him to move, but he wasn't having it. He didn't seem to be in pain, he'd simply run out of energy.

I managed to convince him to get moving after a half-hour break.

He walked down a bit further then he stopped again. In the end, I ditched the gear out of my pack, unzipped it and slid him in, then carried him down this big, steep, slippery hill. At the bottom, he got out and walked quite happily for a kilometre, but then he stopped once more. I ended up carrying him the last 3 kilometres back to the truck. Then I had to head back up the hill and get my gear. I could tell he felt terrible about making all this extra work for me.

It was really sad to see him slow down like that, because he absolutely loves coming out into the bush with me. It started me thinking about what will happen when he can't come out in the field with me so much anymore.

And then something pretty cool happened. In December 2017, I got a call from a contractor working at a forestry site near Motueka. He reckoned there was a kea nest right next to a busy skid site, which is where cut logs are brought to be processed before being trucked out. He said he'd seen some adult kea around the place and that they were acting a bit oddly.

I was a bit sceptical, as kea have never been recorded nesting anywhere other than in native forest, but I figured it would be a good run for Ajax so we headed out to Motueka. When we got there, I soon saw eight kea mucking around in the scrub on the site. That's not unusual, because where there's people, there's food, so they could have just been there to have a bit of a scrounge. Forestry land also has the added bonus of huhu grubs living in the remains of felled trees. Kea will fossick around on the floor of the forest for these little protein-filled treats, and this can lead to quite large social groups of birds spending a lot of time near where trees are being felled.

I went over to where they were and noticed a whole lot of dry sticks and moss just inside the entrance to a drain. I figured that it could have been a nest, so I got Ajax involved. He soon indicated right by the culvert, so I investigated further. Right up in the culvert, around a corner and out of sight, there was a nest—but it was empty.

Ajax was still pretty sure that there were chicks around, though, and he soon disappeared into some scrub next to the culvert. He started to indicate to me that he'd found something. Sure enough,

Me and Ajax still make a great team.

there was a chick sitting there. I grabbed the chick and put it in a bag, ready to be checked and banded. Ajax was still absolutely straining to let me know there was something else he wanted me to check out. Yep, there was a second chick there. Once I had them both, I checked them over, banded them and made my notes. I reckoned they were about two and a half months old.

It was a pretty significant discovery for a few reasons. The main one is that this was the first time that anyone who works with kea had ever found a nest outside of native bush. It was also the first time anyone had found kea nesting in a man-made object in the wild—the culvert.

This just goes to show how adaptable these birds are. We're used to them making use of unnatural food sources, but to nest in an environment that is not natural to them and amidst all the noise and movement of a logging operation is pretty extraordinary. It's also unusual for a kea nest to be discovered by a member of the public like that—I'm really glad the contractor noticed the birds' behaviour and decided to call me out to have a look. A lot of people wouldn't have noticed it.

A couple of days after the nest was found, I went back up there with a group of senior managers from Tasman Pine Forests Ltd, whose patch it was on, to show them where the baby kea were living and to introduce them to Ajax. They loved seeing the birds and have been very supportive of protecting them, temporarily halting operations nearby until the chicks fledged from the nest, which took about a month.

The reason for the shutdown is that as the birds get older, they leave the nest during the day to explore, and they spend a lot more time outside, doing things like flapping their wings in order to build up their muscles for flying. If they had tried to do this around all the vehicles and machinery that were working nearby, it could have been fatal. The work could also have damaged the nest. Thankfully, Tasman Pine Forests was determined this should not happen.

The forestry people were keen to know whether we thought they were going to find more kea, and what they could do to help. Now they know that kea are territorial and that they are likely to return to the same breeding site next year, the culvert is being retained. This is great news, as the company had been planning to redo the road and the culvert would likely have been bulldozed in this process. They are hoping that the birds will return to breed there again.

It's been great to see a company so enthusiastic about having kea found on their property and wanting to help contribute to the conservation of a threatened species. They also loved meeting Ajax, because most people love a dog with a job—and his job is not only to find kea but to help people learn about the birds as well, and he certainly did that out in the forestry.

Part of what made the whole process so easy was the fact that the Kea Conservation Trust worked with the forestry industry for a couple of years to establish a set of kea guidelines for plantation forestry. This was largely brought about as a result of kea causing damage on forestry sites, which had the potential to become a real point of conflict. These guidelines were signed off in early 2017 and have been designed to protect the kea, the forestry workers and any machinery or other material that the kea might take a fancy to. (By the way, one good tip is to smear cinnamon or garlic paste on equipment, because kea don't like the taste of either of those things!)

The guidelines also included what to do if kea were found nesting in a forestry area, though when they were written it was all pretty much theoretical as we'd never seen it happen. Thankfully, we now know that the guidelines work well for everyone involved.

There does seem to be a pattern with kea coming into forestry areas. They'll come in at a certain time of year, stay for a while, then disappear. We don't know where they go for that in-between time and I'd love to find out.

A couple of months after we first found the birds, I went back there to have a look, taking my mum, Sarah, our twins Leo and Zara, and Ajax. We went to the nest site and found the young kea in the trees above the nest, doing well. They've also been seen since—the forestry guys sent me videos of them chewing up some logs. The guys working at the site have really taken to them and they keep an eye on them for me, which is great. It's good to know that they're being looked after. The forestry company is looking at setting up pest control in the area, too, as they've got quite a lot of whio living nearby as well.

Those two young kea will probably hang around the site there for a while, then they'll likely hook up with a flock and take off. I wouldn't expect to see the fledglings again next year, but the parents will probably be there again nesting in that spot.

It's going to be interesting to track these two chicks to see whether they spend all their time near the area where they were born, or whether they'll go off to wherever it is the other birds disappear to and then come back again. I put leg bands on both of them before they left the nest, so we can identify them when they are seen in other places. I didn't put trackers on them at the time, but subsequently one has been taken to the vet with a broken leg, so I will put a transmitter on this one before he is released again.

I'm looking into the possibility of doing more research work around kea in forestry. I reckon it would suit me really well, as now that I've got a young family it's harder to be away from home for long periods of time. As all of the forestry areas are easily accessible, I can drive up to them and Ajax can keep working with less physical exertion. It's a win-win situation.

Not long after the forestry find, I got to go out and meet another population of kea that I hadn't encountered before. In January 2018, I went into Fiordland to do survey work for the first time. The Kea Conservation Trust are working with the Fiordland Wapiti Foundation on the Fiordland Kea Sightings Project, which will help us to monitor kea sightings in their hunting blocks. The foundation runs an annual ballot for members to hunt wapiti, a large deer native to North America, for a ten-day period in March–April each year.

At the end of that hunting period, we've been encouraging them to return information about sightings of kea (or zero reports, if

Ajax takes an opportunity for a snooze in Mount Cook National Park.

they haven't seen any, because that can be significant too). Given they cover around 200,000 hectares of back country, it's a great opportunity for us to get information on part of the country that would be difficult to survey any other way.

Up to 450 hunters gain ballot slots, so there is potential for us to gain a lot of information about kea in the area. This is especially important as there have been anecdotal reports of a declining kea population in Fiordland.

As the plan is to continue the monitoring year on year, it will give us a chance to work out where kea are (and aren't) and what the make-up of the kea population is in terms of juveniles versus adults, and will also give us information on sightings of banded birds. After the 2016 season, we received more than 200 days' worth of data, which has been absolutely invaluable.

The whole project is all about two non-profit organisations working together and trying to establish where the kea are. The same hunters tend to go in there every year, so it's great to get them on board, taking notice of what is happening in the bush and getting them to report back on what they see each time they're out there. It's an important project, because not that much is known about the population status of kea in the Fiordland National Park, which contains lots of prime kea habitat and large tracts of usually unvisited wilderness areas.

In the summer of 2017/2018, as well as getting the wapiti hunters to report back, we went in with some of the guys from the foundation and banded and attached transmitters to a whole lot of birds. There were 14 of us altogether, in four groups, including volunteers from the Fiordland Wapiti Foundation, Ngā Whenua Rāhui and the Department of Conservation. We managed to survey 28 different sites for three hours each evening and again in the morning. All up we caught and banded 44 kea, and two females were fitted with transmitters, which will give us some good information over the next breeding season. This is something we wouldn't have been able to do had we not been able to work alongside the hunting community.

After we got back out of the bush, we had a bit of a yarn about our adventures. All of the kea people had had similar conversations with the different volunteers they were out with. It seemed everyone was interested in the same stuff. The hunters talked a lot about what DOC is doing, and they'd always try to tell us where to go in the bush. They're really experienced in the bush in a hunting capacity, while we're more experienced at getting to the top as quickly as we can. They'd be like, 'Just follow the deer trails!', and we were like, 'Well, deer tend to meander through the forest and you don't really know where the trail is going to lead—and we've got to get up to the top of the mountain!' Given that they're looking for deer, following a deer trail is a good idea, but it's not so useful when you're looking for kea habitat.

Everyone seemed to have a good time. I think the hunters learned a lot from us about why we do what we do. One of the guys with me had some pretty strong opinions on some of the stuff DOC is doing and that's why he decided to come out with us. He wanted to spend some time in the mountains with us so he could ask a lot of questions and try to understand conservationist thinking. That was really good.

The area that we were in was pretty similar to Kahurangi in a lot of ways. There were wide valleys and lots of beech trees, although the hillsides were a bit steeper in places. I thought it was going to be a lot wetter, but the weather was great the whole time. There was a shitload more sandflies down there than anywhere I've been, though, especially at altitude, which was really surprising. They don't normally go that high up in the mountains.

It was a shame that Ajax couldn't come out with me, but the trip was a bit long for him. He did come down to the Hawdon Valley in Arthur's Pass and do a few days of kea surveys with me in January, though, and he did really well, so there's life in the old dog yet.

The great thing about Ajax is that even though he's not as agile as he used to be, he still absolutely loves working. He also really loves people (although happily not so much that he feels

Ajax soaks up the sun on another beaut
day in Kahurangi National Park.

the need to pee on them anymore!). I figure he'll be really happy if I combine those two things and set him to work as an ambassador for both conservation dogs and kea.

A lot of people love dogs, and they love cute dogs more, but what they really love are cute dogs with jobs! On that front, Ajax is the triple threat—a cute dog with an incredibly cool job. Over the years I've been working with him, I've realised that his job isn't just about finding kea, it's also about helping people who might not otherwise have been interested to learn about kea.

While he's been working in this ambassadorial role, Ajax has become something of a film and television star. I guess people have always been pretty interested in Ajax and the work he does, so add that to the fact that he's such a friendly dog and pretty handsome and the media adore him. Sometimes I almost wonder if they're a bit disappointed that they have to talk to me as well!

One of the biggest things he's been involved with in terms of spreading the kea message was the BBC Natural History Unit's documentary *New Zealand: Earth's Mythical Islands*, which screened in the UK in 2016. It was a three-part documentary series narrated by Sam Neill that focused on this country's wildlife and how it had developed through 80 million years of isolation. It was pretty amazing to see Ajax and his work with kea featured in something that was going to be seen all over the world. I'd set up a Facebook page for Ajax—you can find it using the search term @ajaxkea—and each time the show screened it got us a lot more likes, first in the UK and then here in New Zealand. He now has more than 1100 followers and his own Instagram feed (@ajaxthekeadog)!

After spending time with the BBC film crew, I got to thinking about how it would be good to make a show just about Ajax. I talked to my mate Michael Weatherall, who is a film-maker who's done a lot of work with international film crews in the South Island and also for the Kea Conservation Trust. I told him that all these film crews seemed to be keen on Ajax and that he should make a film about the dog.

He was really keen on the idea, too, so together with producer

Cecilia Shand, he put together a proposal for the Loading Docs initiative, which is run by New Zealand On Air, Te Māngai Pāho and the New Zealand Film Commission. They select ten proposals for short documentaries each year, and work with the film-makers right from the development stage through to production, promotion and distribution. The stories that get picked have to have the potential to 'captivate and inspire both nationally and internationally', so it was pretty sweet when Michael (and Ajax) got selected to join the programme.

That meant that we would get $4000 in funding to make the documentary, but we also needed to raise an extra $2000 on top of that, so Michael set up a Boosted page to seek crowdfunding. We hoped to get an extra $2000 but we ended up having 130 people donate money, and we raised just over $6000! The whole team was delighted with that, as it meant we could do that much more to get the shots we needed, including hiring a helicopter to get some mint aerial footage.

We took three or four days to shoot the film. I managed to take Michael to some pretty spectacular locations around Kahurangi to show him what a normal working day is like for Ajax. We even managed to get some good sunny weather and a bitterly cold windy day, for a bit of variety. We went through streams, over wire bridges, down kea nests, up mountains—the works—to show what we do for work. And yes, we did manage to find a kea for Michael to film. And you only need to watch the film to know that Ajax was a complete natural in front of the camera!

There was so much great footage that I don't know how Michael and the team managed to cut it down to just over three minutes, but the film they made is beautiful and it's certainly helped get the message about Ajax and kea out there to a lot of people since it was released.

One of the great things about the Loading Docs films is that they're freely available for people to share online, so it's gone all around the world and got us heaps of attention from different media outlets. Ajax's story has been seen in film festivals in New

Zealand, Australia and the United States, and featured on plenty of conservation websites, including National Geographic, which is pretty amazing.

As well as the short film and the BBC documentary, Ajax has also featured on TVNZ's *Sunday* programme and on *Dog Squad*, which is all about dogs with jobs. Most of the other dogs on that show are city dogs that spend their time picking up people who are trying to evade police, smuggle drugs or bring illegal products into the country, so having Ajax out in the bush finding kea, including two tiny chicks, made for a nice change.

I've also been interviewed about Ajax on Kim Hill's Saturday morning show on Radio New Zealand National, and there's been stories about him in magazines such as *Say Yes to Adventure*, *Latitude* and *New Zealand Geographic*.

Every bit of coverage we get helps get the word out there about kea, so being a media star is now a big part of Ajax's job. I just have to be sure not to let the fame go to his head!

Another important part of Ajax's job that he loves is going to schools to teach kids about kea. When I was a kid, a local man who had a guide dog brought him into school. I remember that day so clearly—it was so cool to have a dog in our classroom. I know that Ajax will be just as memorable to the kids that I take him to visit. The kids really engage with him. They can relate to him because they've maybe got a dog at home or they've been around other people's dogs, but at the same time they probably never imagined that a dog could have a job. Seeing as we can't take the birds themselves into schools, taking Ajax is the next best thing for encouraging kids to become passionate about saving kea.

Quite often, when I take him into a classroom, I'll hide him somewhere first—under some desks at the back of the room or in the porch outside. The kids will all come in and sit down, then I'll stand in front of the class and talk about kea and conservation. Right when they're starting to glaze over a wee bit, I'll give a bit of a whistle. Running from the back of the classroom, right through all the kids, comes Ajax. They absolutely love it!

I do ask the kids if anyone is scared of dogs first, and I had one kid say he was. I assured him that Ajax would be fine. The kid freaked out a bit but then gradually calmed down and soon came to love him. That's the good thing about Ajax being so calm. He just can't understand it when he meets people—especially kids—who don't like dogs. Most people love him, so when he meets people who are scared of him or seem to dislike him, he's not sure what to do with himself. He'll sit and look at them and try to work out how to deal with them.

As Ajax slows down a bit more, it'll be great to spend more time taking him into classrooms and doing educational work.

As well as his kea work, Ajax has another job that he takes very seriously. Sarah and I had twins in late 2017, then got married in early 2018, so we've been pretty busy. Ajax has been in the thick of all of it, of course. He's a working dog but he's also very much part of the family.

He takes his new job of looking after the kids very seriously. That said, he's a bit jealous of them as well. You can tell he doesn't particularly like them and he's waiting for them to leave. He's got a long wait! He doesn't like not being the centre of attention too much, but he's getting used to it. They're starting to pat him a wee bit and play with his ears. Once he realises that they're a good source of pats then he'll be real happy.

He also had an important role to play at our wedding—and as usual he almost stole the show. We got married in St Arnaud, and Ajax played a bit of a starring role. Of course, with the rest of us all dressed up he couldn't be left out, so he wore a vest and a bow tie the whole night. He's so used to being handled and me chucking clothes on him when he's cold that he didn't mind getting dressed up—although this was the first time that he's had to wear a bow tie.

At the ceremony, when the celebrant said, 'Does anyone know any reason why these two should not be wed?', Ajax stood up and walked over to us and stared at me with a curious look on his face!

Ajax with our twins,
Leonardo and Zara.

It was really funny timing. No wonder people can't tell if he's my sidekick or I'm his!

After that, he spent quite a lot of time annoying the people doing the catering and making friends where he could. He loved all the attention. He was out and about cruising until about midnight, which is a late night for a dog that's usually in bed by ten!

I sometimes think about how my life would have turned out if it hadn't been for Tamsin spotting that Catahoula listing on TradeMe all those years ago, or if Ajax hadn't passed all his tests to become an accredited conservation dog. Although I'm passionate about kea and I love working with them, I probably wouldn't have kept working with them if I hadn't had Ajax by my side.

While Ajax is incredibly useful in the field, he also makes the job way more enjoyable for me. It's great to have Ajax's company, especially when I'm out in the field for long periods of time. He's a super chilled-out companion, he's always happy to see me (except first thing in the morning if the sun isn't quite up!) and he regularly provides me with entertainment.

But while working with Ajax has changed my life, it's probably had more of an impact on the lives of kea in this country. While our work monitoring the nests doesn't actually increase the population of kea directly, it helps researchers to understand what's happening to the birds in the field. By increasing that understanding, we have increased the ability to work out exactly what can be done to ensure that the kea population not only remains stable but that it grows in the future.

As well as getting more information on what's happening with kea, Ajax's work has also helped a lot of people understand the work that dogs do in conservation. Some people are still a bit suspicious when they see Ajax out in a national park, as they see dogs as being a predatory threat. That's slowly changing as more people come to understand how dogs like Ajax are trained and how they work.

When Ajax and I started working together, I didn't expect him to be able to do half the stuff he's done. I've learned from that, and through what I've learned I can help other people to understand just what these dogs are capable of.

All of the work we've done together aside, it's hard to believe that that little puppy that peed all over my car, was scared of hedgehogs and that hated getting out of bed in the morning turned out to be one of the best mates I've ever had. I can't imagine anyone else that I could have spent as much time with and had as many adventures with than good old Ajax.

A juvenile male kea in Mount Cook National Park.

APPENDIX 1:
ABOUT THE KEA
CONSERVATION TRUST

By Tamsin Orr-Walker

I was one of the founders of the trust in 2006, when I was working as a keeper at Auckland Zoo. Since then, I've moved south to Queenstown to be a bit closer to the birds. In setting up the trust, our main goals were to assist with the conservation of wild kea in their natural habitat, and to ensure that kea in captivity are advocated for and maintained to a high standard.

In terms of wild kea conservation, our work is done through establishing good relationships with other conservation groups; raising funds for research into issues affecting kea, in particular with regard to habitat and predation; and providing plenty of easily accessible information about the birds.

For captive birds, we provide advice on how best to manage captive populations, and raise funds for research into enclosure design and maintaining the birds in the best physical and psychological condition possible.

We work with a group of advisors who collectively have a massive amount of knowledge about kea. Education is a key part of our work, so we have a very active Facebook community, bi-monthly email newsletters and a website full of kea-related information. On top of that, we have staff and volunteers available to give community talks and presentations, and we have produced some great resources for schools.

Talking to children is always a good gauge of what the community is thinking. Children listen to what their parents are saying and they'll mimic it. On the West Coast of the South Island, we'd ask kids what they knew about kea. They'd say that they're really naughty and always doing bad things. I'd say to the kids, 'I remember when I was a kid, my brother wanted to find out how a clock worked, so he opened my parents' clock up and pulled it apart and he couldn't get it back together again. How many of you have done something you didn't mean to do?' The stories would start flowing about things these kids had done without meaning any harm. I'd say to them, 'That's just like being a kea. They're explorers and they want to understand their environment. They don't mean to be naughty!' You can see the kids' eyes light up when they really get it. Some of the parents must hate me for turning their kids into kea warriors!

We have strong relationships with local community groups, including DOC, scientific and conservation groups, tourism operators, high-country farming communities, schools, tertiary facilities, local communities and zoos. Additionally, a large pool of enthusiastic volunteers provides 3000 hours of operational, field, education and scientific expertise every year.

In 2008, one of those enthusiastic volunteers was Corey. He came down from Whanganui to help out on a kea population survey we were doing in Mount Aspiring National Park. He was really enthusiastic about what we were doing and, on top of that, he was pretty persistent about wanting to work with the birds. That's the best way to get into working in conservation in this country.

Working with volunteers is a really good way of getting to know people and getting people engaged with the trust. Working with him in the kea environment was a great way to see how much Corey had to offer.

We managed to get funding to start doing the kea population surveys, so we contracted Corey to do some work with one of our field advisors, Josh Kemp. Eventually, Corey became our field research co-ordinator.

When Corey started talking about getting a dog, I realised how beneficial a kea dog would be for the work that he does. I'd taken an interest in Catahoulas years ago because they're such a fascinating breed. I ended up getting a dog that was full Catahoula and they're such good nose dogs—they're great with rescue work and hunting, so there seemed to be good potential there for them to do bird work.

I had an alert set up on TradeMe so that if anyone listed anything with Catahoula in it, I'd get an email. When I got a notification that someone was giving away pups that were Catahoulas crossed with border collie, who are renowned for their smarts, I rang Corey and said, 'Go and get him!'

Ajax is the first dog to have been trained specifically for finding kea. There are other dogs that have been trained for multiple species, but he's the first solely kea dog. Having him on the team has made a huge difference to the work that we do.

It's just a fantastic partnership between Ajax and Corey. Finding a kea nest is a needle-in-a-haystack scenario, and the haystack might be knee-deep in snow with a major weather event expected any minute! But still Ajax gets in there and gets the job done. I think he's hugely proved his worth over the years. The other benefit for Corey is having companionship when he is out in the mountains by himself for long periods of time.

Ajax is used to being in lots of different situations with lots of different people. When we go out on surveys, he's around an awful lot of other people. Everyone likes to have Ajax in their tent. He provides them with company, and a bit of added warmth on cold nights as well! I've had him in my tent before and he's lovely to cuddle up to.

He's very adaptable and unflappable, which is a handy trait for a bird dog. He has always been a really balanced dog, and that makes him a convincing ambassador for the birds. It's great that Corey's been able to take him into schools, as there's nothing that will get kids more excited about conservation than having Ajax come in and visit them. Everyone wants to meet him and pat him. It's especially useful given that we can't take birds into the schools for the kids to meet—meeting the dog and hearing about the work he does helps them understand that kea need help.

The thing about dogs is that everyone can relate to how great it is to have a dog. Kids can identify with how it feels for Corey to work with Ajax.

Every time we have Ajax on our Facebook page, we get heaps of attention. Add a kea to the picture and you've got the ultimate in content. People just love seeing him with the birds. Through that alone, he's doing wonders for kea conservation.

In October 2017, the kea was voted Bird of the Year in an annual competition put on by Forest & Bird. Given there were 168 birds in the running, we were thrilled to take the win. It was quite funny, as we were getting calls from journalists overseas who couldn't work out why people here were getting so into the contest—especially when they found out there were no prizes! I would explain that it was all about raising awareness and that it was incredibly valuable from a conservation perspective—even if there was no money in it.

There was great teamwork involved in winning that one for the kea. Corey and Laura Young, one of our other bird handlers, made a couple of 'vote for kea' videos up on top of a mountain. Making the videos out in the field helped people to understand the work we do, with the added bonus of letting them see the birds, Ajax and some pretty spectacular scenery. Those videos really got people voting for kea. It was brilliant.

One of the biggest hurdles we face is the fact that people find it difficult to understand how few kea there are. We do the rounds of the ski fields and ask them to give us a yell when they see kea. They all tell us the same thing—the first day of the season, they won't see any kea; the second day, word will get around and they'll be there. Whenever there's human activity somewhere, kea suddenly descend on that place. It's largely because they're attracted by the activity, but also because they know they're going to get food. The problem with this is that people who see them then assume that there are heaps of kea around, when actually there's just a very small number that are very mobile.

One of our main projects is around conflict resolution. We recognise that kea can be a massive headache for people, so helping to reduce conflict situations is a big part of what we do. We want to be able to work with people to help them and to help the birds.

Kea have had a long history of persecution in New Zealand. The perception that kea are pests persists to this day, but a pest is actually an introduced, non-native species that has a negative impact on our ecosystems—it's definitely not one of our beautiful native birds. We want people to change the way they look at kea. We'd like them to understand that it's a real privilege to have these birds around.

One of our challenges comes with the changing use of land in some high-country areas. A lot of land that used to be farmland is now being sold and converted into housing estates, golf courses, luxury hotels and the like. We do our best to work with the people who are moving into kea-habitat areas to make sure they understand the role of the birds and the risks that are associated with them. One of the problems is that these new people coming in and building are creating fascinating places, full of new things for kea to investigate.

We've done quite a lot of work with farmers, too, and it's always great when they come to us for help when they're having issues with kea. That willingness to ask for help is a hugely positive step, especially seeing it wasn't that long ago that farmers would have just shot the birds for being a nuisance.

Back when many of the farms in the high country were created, kea habitat in the form of bushland was destroyed in order to sow grass and graze sheep, which then became a food source for the birds. The fact that people were paid a bounty to destroy kea is a dark part of our history, and people don't really like to talk too much about it. Nor do people like to admit that they're having issues with kea. For some farmers, there's a perception that they don't want 'a bunch of greenies' getting involved in their business, so we do our best to assure them that we want what's best both for them and for the birds. It's a topic that's incredibly controversial.

We have had conflict situations where people blame kea for everything that happens on their property. We had one case near Queenstown where a woman called us because she didn't want kea around her house—despite the fact that she claimed to love native birds. She had two juveniles that were making a bit of a mess around her place, digging up pansies and winding up her two indoor cats by sitting just outside the window.

She was convinced that they were also pushing over plant pots at night and doing all sorts of other stuff. I set up some cameras around the place and found that most of the damage was being done by possums. Her next-door neighbour's cats were in on the mischief as well. After that, it was very difficult for her to argue that the kea were the main culprits! Yes, they were causing a bit of strife, but she was blaming them for a lot more than they were actually doing.

There's conflict between humans and wildlife the world over. In September 2017 I went to a conference about the space where humans and animals clash, accompanied by our conflict resolution specialist, Andrea Goodman. There were people from Africa having issues with elephants, people from the United States working with wolves and bears, people from Belize working with sharks—the conference covered the whole spectrum of animal groups from around the world, and the story was the same with every single one: it was all about intolerance and fear. It made me realise how lucky we are that kea don't actually threaten people's lives—unlike some of the endangered animals that other people were there advocating for.

The one thing every situation had in common was that humans were moving further and further into the habitat of these creatures and competing with them for resources. If we didn't have kea, then we wouldn't have a planet that was fit for any species to survive in— they're incredibly intelligent and adaptable, so if they die out then it's a pretty dire sign for the planet.

At home in New Zealand, our work with farmers continues. On one site we visited, we ended up using a kea repellent that we've been involved in developing—we applied it onto the backs of their sheep. This farm said that they'd usually have about 40 sheep deaths a year that they associated with kea, but this particular year they reckoned there had been 400. They didn't actually have any bodies of the sheep for us to inspect—these animals just hadn't come in during the muster.

I went out with one of our researchers for a couple of days and we travelled all over the station doing an audit of bird numbers and looking for any problems. We found Pink Batts that had been soaked in fat and put out in a back paddock. The kea would have been attracted by the fat and, when they ate it, they would have ingested the glass wool, which would have caused them a very slow and painful death. Sadly, this used to be a favoured way for farmers to kill kea. The Pink Batts were very old and they'd clearly been up there for a long time, but someone must have known that they were still there. We only found one breeding pair of kea on the whole property, so the likelihood of them killing that many sheep was pretty much zero.

It's very difficult to get people to be rational when they've been told by previous generations that kea are doing all the damage. They don't need evidence because they just *know*. There could have been a million things that killed those sheep, but they chose to believe that it was the birds.

I can't sing Ajax and Corey's praises highly enough—not only for the fieldwork and the direct kea work that they do, but for the whole advocacy side of things as well. They get people engaged, at all age levels, which has been absolutely wonderful both for the trust and for the birds.

An adult male kea blends in with his surrounds at Klondyke Corner in Canterbury.

APPENDIX 2:
WAYS YOU CAN HELP KEA

1. Report any sightings of kea

You can report sightings on the Kea Database website (www. keadatabase.nz) or you can contact your nearest DOC office. Even better, submit photos of your sighting. Helpful details to include in your report are the date, time and location of the sighting, as well as whether the bird was banded—if so, include the colour combination or numbers on the bands if visible, and note what the kea was doing when you spotted it. While you're online, check out some more of the kea that have been tagged, named and sighted around the country.

2. Discourage kea from interacting with humans

If there are kea around, make sure you don't leave tempting items where the birds can get them—this includes food, packs, clothing, boots and any brightly coloured objects.

If you have a property in the Southern Alps, investigate whether there is lead in any of the roofing (especially nails) or flashing. If there is, replace it with non-toxic alternatives.

Don't feed kea. Ever. Anything. Feeding the birds is harmful to them for a number of reasons—it attracts them to where humans are, putting them at risk of being run over or purposefully harmed, it changes their feeding habits, and the food itself can be harmful to their digestive systems.

3. Report any incidents that may be causing harm to the birds

Call 0800 DOC HOT (0800 362 468) immediately if you see anyone setting traps, threatening to shoot, catching, harming or killing kea (or any other native wildlife).

4. Support the Kea Conservation Trust

The trust's main aim is to assist in conservation of wild kea in their natural habitat, and to ensure the future of both wild and captive kea populations. They do this by working with other conservation groups, raising funds for research and making sure people can easily access plenty of information about kea. They also advocate for kea held in captive facilities in New Zealand.

The trust is a registered charity, and through donations they fund important work to secure the future of these amazing birds, including a lot of the work Ajax and I do tracking kea. Check out their website at: www.keaconservation.co.nz.

5. Do what you can in your everyday life to be mindful of the environment and of local populations of wildlife

Some great things to do for kea, and all other native bird species, are:

- Take your dog on an avian awareness course. This will help to teach your dog to leave all birds alone.
- Get involved in local initiatives to control predators such as rats, stoats, possums and hedgehogs. Most cities now have pest-control projects in certain areas, so don't think living in town gets you out of helping! Better still, set some predator traps on your own property.
- If you have cats, make sure they're well-fed and, if necessary, put a bell on your cat's collar to warn birds when it's around. If possible, keep your cats indoors at night.
- Obey any requests not to take dogs into areas where they're not allowed. Even if you think your dog is particularly well behaved, you don't want to risk it killing an endangered bird when you're not looking.

6. Talk to DOC or the Kea Conservation Trust

They're always happy to advise you about how to kea-proof your home, what to do if you find a dead kea, or what to do if you think kea are at risk near you. Don't take things into your own hands—for your sake and for the birds'.

An adult female kea with her eggs
in Nelson Lakes National Park.

A peaceful scene at Kahurangi National Park.

APPENDIX 3: RESOLVING CONFLICT WITH KEA

Courtesy of the Kea Conservation Trust

Today the perception of kea as destructive and a nuisance still persists. Changes in land use and increasing human activity and access into high-country areas are resulting in kea coming into contact with more people and their property. For example, Fiordland National Park, one of New Zealand's most pristine wilderness areas, and Arthur's Pass, home to our most visible population of kea, host around 500,000 visitors annually.

Property damage is reported each year by private landowners (including sheep farmers), tourists, tourist operators and workers, and many more kea conflict events may go unreported. Modifying wild kea behaviour has proven to be difficult. Kea are hard-wired to be curious about new things in their environment and are destructive with items they are able to manipulate.

While kea behaviour can be destructive and annoying, unlike in other countries conflict with our wildlife is not life-threatening to people. It can, however, be life-threatening for kea. Every year a number of kea are found shot, intentionally injured or poisoned as a result of conflict with humans.

Resolving conflict is therefore largely about re-educating local communities about kea (status, numbers, uniqueness), kea behaviour (why they damage property, kea attractants, kea deterrents), and people's own behaviour and practices around kea. In some cases this has resulted in better understanding of the issues facing kea and the role of local communities in protecting the birds.

Ongoing human–kea conflict is a challenge which is imperative to solve. While there is conflict, there is the potential for negative perceptions of the species to be retained and kea to be illegally killed.

Kea are a fully protected species, and to harm or remove kea from an area without a permit is illegal.

To help with this, the Kea Conservation Trust has developed a proactive, community-focused conflict response and resolution programme. This project received funding mid-2014 and was initiated in the Motueka/Tasman/Nelson area. It has subsequently been rolled out across the South Island.

This project aims to identify the nature of conflict experienced by people living within kea habitat, provide 'first response' during conflict situations, help people be proactive to prevent problem situations arising, and research practical methods of conflict resolution, in collaboration and partnership with affected individuals, communities and DOC.

Why are kea so destructive?

Kea are neophilic—they love exploring anything new. This is an evolutionary response developed over millions of years of living in an extreme environment. They are therefore attracted to human activity and belongings. Anything that is able to be manipulated (soft and pliable) is of particular interest, and anything which provides a food reward is of even more interest (e.g. food inside a styrofoam container or bin). There has been some research to suggest that certain colours attract kea, in particular white, yellow and red.

What do I do if I have a problem with kea?

The trust recognises that curious kea can cause significant damage to human property. If you experience any problems which you need positive help and support solving, contact the Kea Conservation Trust, who will work with you to bring about a good result for both you and the birds. Conflict situations can be reported via the website (www.keaconservation.co.nz) or by email.

What will the trust do?

The Conflicts Response Programme (funded by DOC and Cincinnati Zoo and Botanical Gardens) provides the following resources to help communities resolve kea conflict while protecting remnant kea populations:

- On-the-ground support during conflict events, including free on-site assessment and reporting of the situation, trialling of kea-repellent options and kea-proofing areas (where practicable and as funding allows), and ongoing support until the situation is resolved.
- A conflicts database, to record kea issues and track the process of resolution.
- An advice package for people with conflict issues, to provide people experiencing issues with information on what they can do and who they can contact.

In addition to this, the programme provides the trust with the ability to:

- Undertake ongoing research into methods of conflict resolution.
- Appoint key people within affected communities to be its 'eyes and ears' for kea.
- Encourage community-led kea conservation initiatives to resolve conflict in key areas

What can I do?

Contact the trust if you have any issues with kea. They can't help if they don't know about it!

Complete a survey form if you have ever had or are having conflict issues with kea. Information from past situations might help the trust better understand ways of resolving specific issues or other factors (such as season, weather, human activity) which are encouraging the birds. This information will form the basis of the conflicts database.

The trust needs sites where it can trial different kea-deterrent options. If you are having regular issues with kea and are happy to be involved in a trial, please contact the trust.

Get in touch with the trust if you are happy to be our eyes and ears in your community. You can alert us to any conflict situations in the community that the trust may not be aware of, or supply details of any human behaviour which may be contributing to situations.

Contact us if you can keep an eye out for kea. Some people continue to kill kea or threaten to do so, and we need to know if this is likely to occur or has occurred.

Help the trust to help you—it is a charity and has limited funds. The trust does not charge for its time but appreciate your support when resolving kea conflict situations. Accommodation and a warm welcome are enormously appreciated!

If you have had problems with kea and found solutions to these issues, please complete a kea-proofing form on the trust's website (www.keaconservation.co.nz/support-kea/kea-proofing). This will help others experiencing the same issues.

And finally, please be tolerant of kea—they were here long before any people arrived in New Zealand and they have a right to live here, too.

It is important to remember that many communities throughout the South Island do live conflict-free with kea. It can be done and is generally only a matter of making a few changes in the way that you live and/or protect your property.

Kea-proofing your home

General tips

- Ensure your home is as unattractive to kea as possible. This way they may well leave a property alone and cause minimal damage.
- Don't leave anything lying around outside that can be damaged.
- If you can't put something away, cover any vulnerable areas with a kea-proof cover.
- Close all doors and windows when you vacate the premises.
- Ensure all rubbish bins are securely closed at all times.
- Don't feed kea—it only takes one instance to encourage kea to revisit a site.
- Ask any visitors to your property not to feed kea.

A juvenile kea tells Ajax what's what at Death's Corner.

Ajax rests up in preparation for another
adventure at Mount Cook National Park.

- Take care when disposing of food scraps so that kea can't get into them.
- Feed pets inside where possible and dispose of any uneaten pet food, as kea will be able to sniff out leftover dog roll or cat biscuits.
- Don't set up bird feeders, even when kea aren't around, as they will be attracted by the free food.
- Do not bang on ceilings, yell or throw things at kea, as this will only make them more curious.
- Use a garden hose to move kea off areas—but be accurate so it doesn't become a 'game' to them.
- Use deterrents such as bird spikes to keep kea off roof areas.
- Cover any soft materials that may attract kea (such as outdoor-seating cushions, bicycle seats, polystyrene, exposed wiring and hosing) with tarpaulins or netting.
- Reduce access to any potential roosting areas.
- Put all children's/pet toys away to reduce interest.
- Cover compost areas with a net/tarpaulin.
- Keep your outside area as tidy as possible—the more untidy an area is, the more interesting it becomes!

Wiring/electrical equipment
- Where possible, all wires should be covered so they are not exposed to kea.
- Cover any electrical plugs.

Windows and doors (including vehicles)
- Keep windows and doors shut at all times.
- Block any access areas with plywood sheets or tarpaulins.

Other pollutants
- Remove (i.e. do not simply throw under a building) all potential pollutants such as old batteries or lead roofing.
- Ensure all rubbish is kept in covered rubbish bins, and remove it from the property on a regular basis.

Kea-proofing your work site

General tips

- Ensure the site is as unattractive to kea as possible. This way they may well leave a work site alone and cause minimal damage.
- Ensure all crew and visitors to the site are aware that they should never feed kea—it only takes one instance to encourage kea to revisit a site. Do not throw food scraps into the surrounding bush or chuck anything out vehicle windows (even when kea are not around).
- Cover any soft materials that may attract kea (such as seats, polystyrene, exposed wiring and hosing) with tarpaulins or netting.
- Ensure no rubbish is left lying around.
- Reduce access to any potential roosting areas.

Wiring/electrical equipment

- Where possible, secure all wires in places where kea cannot gain access to them.
- Place flexible metal ducting over exposed wires.
- Cover any electrical plugs.

Windows and doors (including work vehicles)

- Keep windows and doors shut at all times.
- Block any access areas with plywood sheets or tarpaulins.

Pink Batts and other insulation

- Cover insulation at all times when building is in progress.
- Ensure no access is possible for kea.

Other pollutants

- Remove (i.e. do not simply throw under a building) all potential pollutants such as old batteries or lead roofing.
- Ensure all rubbish is kept in covered rubbish bins, and remove it from the site on a regular basis.

If kea start becoming a nuisance

If kea start causing damage to items on the site, in the first instance contact either the Kea Conservation Trust (info@keaconservation. co.nz; 0274 249 594) or DOC.

BIBLIOGRAPHY

Books

Chambers, S., *Birds of New Zealand*, Arun Books, Orewa, 2009.

Diamond, J. and Bond, A., *Kea: bird of paradox*, University of California Press, Berkeley, 1999.

Gill, B. J. et al., *Checklist of the Birds of New Zealand, Norfolk and Macquarie Islands, and the Ross Dependency, Antarctica*, Te Papa Press, Wellington, 2010.

Heather, B. and Robertson, H., *The Field Guide to Birds of New Zealand*, Penguin Books, Auckland, 2005.

Higgins, P. J. (ed.), *Handbook of Australian, New Zealand and Antarctic Birds*, Oxford University Press, Melbourne, 1999.

Marriner, G. R., *The Kea: a New Zealand problem*, Marriner Bros & Co., Christchurch, 1908.

Watola, G., *The Discovery of New Zealand Birds*, Arun Books, Orewa, 2009.

Journal and other articles

Brown, G., 'Big brother boosts bird breeding', *The Press*, 21 June 2009.

Cheyne, J., 'Protected species and predator detection dog use in New Zealand wildlife conservation projects', *New Zealand Journal of Ecology*, 2011, vol. 35 (2): pp. 192–193.

Clark, F., 'Tree nettle (*Urtica ferox*) poisoning', *New Zealand Medical Journal*, June 1993, vol. 106 (957): p. 234.

Clarke, C. M. H., 'Observations on population, movements and food of the kea (*Nestor notabilis*)', *Notornis*, 1970, vol. 17, pp. 105–114.

Elliot, G. and Kemp, J., 'Effect of hunting and predation on kea, and a method of monitoring kea populations', DOC Science

Internal Series 181, Department of Conservation, Wellington, 2004.

Fletcher, J., 'Motorists urged to be vigilant after two kea found dead in Arthur's Pass', *The Press*, 21 August 2016.

Foundation for Research Science and Technology, 'Kiwi Saver Hits the Mark', www.scoop.co.nz, 1 May 2008.

Gee, S., 'Kea nest discovered in culvert on Motueka forestry site hailed as significant', www.stuff.co.nz, 24 December 2017.

Gould, J., 'On two new species of birds (*Nestor notabilis* and *Spatula variegata*) from the collection of Walter Mantell, Esq.', *Proceedings of the Zoological Society of London*, 1856, vol. 24: pp. 94–95.

Heaney, M., Gray, R. and Taylor, A., 'Keas perform similarly to chimpanzees and elephants when solving collaborative tasks', 2017, *PLOS ONE* 12 (2), doi.org/10.1371/journal.pone.0169799.

Kea Conservation Trust/New Zealand Forest Owners Association, 'Kea guidelines for plantation forestry', rarespecies.nzfoa.org.nz/site/assets/files/1088/final_kea_guidelines_at_5_may_pp.pdf.

Mills, L., 'Established benchmark in island conservation', *Otago Daily Times*, 31 August 2015.

Nicholl, D., 'Roadcone-moving kea get gym to distract them away from traffic', www.stuff.co.nz, 10 January 2018.

Pearson, A., 'Daredevil kea score new playground in Arthur's Pass', *The Press*, 19 February 2015.

Robertson, H. A. et al., 'Conservation status of New Zealand birds, 2016', New Zealand Threat Classification Series 19, Department of Conservation, Wellington.

Rykers, E., 'Track and Trace', *New Zealand Geographic*, vol. 149, Jan–Feb 2018.

Temple, P., 'Kea: the feisty parrot', *New Zealand Geographic*, vol. 24, Oct–Dec 1994.

White, R., 'The rarest of the rare,' *New Zealand Geographic*, vol. 138, Mar–Apr 2016.

Websites

Keane, K., 'Ngā manu—birds—Birds' names', Te Ara—the Encyclopedia of New Zealand, www.teara.govt.nz/en/nga-manu-birds/page-6 (accessed 29 March 2018).

Kemp, J., 'Kea', New Zealand Birds Online, www.nzbirdsonline.org.nz/species/kea.

Messerli Research Institute, 'Kea Lab', University of Veterinary Medicine, www.vetmeduni.ac.at/en/messerli/science/cognition/wildlife/kea-lab.

Wassilieff, M., 'Poisonous plants and fungi—Poisonous native plants', Te Ara—the Encyclopedia of New Zealand, www.teara.govt.nz/en/poisonous-plants-and-fungi/page-1 (accessed 21 March 2018).

Additional image credits

(All photography by Corey Mosen unless otherwise credited.)

Pages 2–3: Ajax on the job in Mount Aspiring National Park.

Pages 4–5: A juvenile kea in Arthur's Pass National Park.

Pages 6–7: Kahurangi National Park is like a second home to Ajax.

Pages 8–9: Ajax on White Horse Hill in Mount Cook National Park.

Pages 10–11: Ajax and Sarah check out different vantage points in Kahurangi National Park.

Pages 18–19: A quiet moment for Ajax in the Wairau Valley.

Pages 34–35: Another stunning day in Kahurangi National Park.

Pages 54–55: Ajax and I enjoy the early evening light in Kahurangi National Park. PHOTO BY JANE TAYLOR

Pages 64–65: Ajax hitches a lift with me across a swing bridge in Kahurangi National Park. PHOTO BY LINDSAY SKYNER

Pages 92–93: Wearing the high-vis gear doesn't bother Ajax as he cruises around in Kahurangi National Park.

Pages 108–109: A well-earned break for Ajax in Kahurangi National Park.

Pages 120–121: It's rest time for Ajax while I check for signals in the Wairau Valley. PHOTO BY LINDSAY SKYNER

Pages 138–139: Ajax checks a kea nest in Kahurangi National Park.

Pages 160–161: A dining companion has joined Ajax in Kahurangi National Park.

Pages 170–171: Kahurangi National Park is the scene of another day at the office for Ajax.

Pages 188–189: Ajax quickly became a pro at negotiating fast-moving rivers.

Pages 200–201: Ajax looks on as I take a bath in a frozen tarn at Kahurangi National Park. PHOTO BY MATT CHARTERIS

Pages 212–213: Me and Sarah (and Ajax!) on our wedding day in St Arnaud. PHOTO BY TASMAN PHOTOGRAPHY